T0195267

TO

_____

FROM

_____

DATE

_____

# CATCH A BETTER LIFE

## DAILY DEVOTIONS & FISHING TIPS

# JIMMY HOUSTON

COUNTRYMAN®

An Imprint of Thomas Nelson Publishers

THOMAS NELSON

*Since 1798*

Published in Nashville, Tennessee, by Thomas Nelson. Thomas Nelson is a registered trademark of HarperCollins Christian Publishing, Inc.

Lure photography by Jeremy Combs
Cover illustrated by Kathy Mitchell
Cover photos by OMS Photography, Inc. and Leslee Mitchell
Interior design by Kristy Edwards

Thomas Nelson titles may be purchased in bulk for educational, business, fund-raising, or sales promotional use. For information, please email SpecialMarkets@ ThomasNelson.com.

Unless otherwise noted, Scripture quotations are taken from the New King James Version®. Copyright © 1982 by Thomas Nelson. Used by permission. All rights reserved.

Scripture quotations marked CEV are from the Contemporary English Version. Copyright © 1991, 1992, 1995 by American Bible Society. Used by permission.

ISBN 978-1-4002-2933-8 (audiobook)
ISBN 978-1-4002-2931-4 (eBook)
ISBN 978-1-4002-2932-1 (HC)

*Printed in India*

22 23 24 25 26 BPI 10 9 8 7 6 5 4 3 2 1

JANUARY

GENESIS 1:20

*God said, "Let the waters abound with an abundance of living creatures."*

**W**e all love to fish waters that are teeming with fish. When I first fished the Thousand Islands area on the St. Lawrence River, I could not believe how many bass were there. If it was a good-looking spot, there was a bass there. You could actually call your shot. It was like speaking a bass into existence.

In fact, God did exactly that. He spoke everything into existence: land, water, animals, and yes, fish! Wouldn't that be an awesome power to have? Well, you have it; you can speak joy into others' lives by saying something nice—you can speak courage into your kids and friends with words of encouragement. Speak health and peace with prayer and understanding words to people who are hurting. You can speak love with a simple smile. Speak something great into existence today.

**TIP**

The lower end of lakes—near a dam—is usually better in the cold winter months.

PROVERBS 3:9–10
*Honor the Lord with your possessions . . . so
your barns will be filled with plenty.*

The key to being successful in tournament fishing, or just fishing, period, is preparation and commitment. For a pro angler, it is a three-day official practice that creates success or failure. We work daylight until dark those three days in all types of weather and harsh conditions. Why? To have success during the actual tournament days!

One key to being a successful Christian is tithing—honoring God with what He has provided us. When we honor God with what we have, He will fill our barns with plenty! And we know we can't outgive God. Obviously, our possessions are not just money. We also honor God with our time and talents. And the plenty that God fills our barns with is also more than money. It is joy, peace, health, wisdom, favor, understanding—and more. Honor God today with what you have, and watch your barns overflow.

**TIP**
Use marker buoys to lay out creek channels in open water.

# JANUARY 3

PSALM 27:8

*When you said, "Seek My face," my heart said*
*to You, "Your face, LORD, I will seek."*

Tournament fishermen tend to cover every part of their bodies with masks, gloves, and long sleeves to protect themselves from the sun. It is all but impossible to recognize any of them on the water. At one time during the coronavirus pandemic, my wife, Chris, went into our bank. Later she said, "I feel really funny walking into a bank wearing a mask." I'd imagine!

God asks us to seek His face. He doesn't wear a mask. He is asking us to get personal with Him. He wants believers to have a personal, one-on-one relationship with Him. Think about that. The God who created the universe and flung the stars into existence wants to be involved in everything we do. If your relationship with God is long-distance, not personal, ask Him to come into your heart, and make Him Lord of your life.

**TIP**
Small hair jigs fished under a bobber are great in clear, cold water.

NUMBERS 11:17

*"I will take of the Spirit that is upon you
and will put the same upon them."*

Tournament fishermen often work with one or two other pros and share information about how to catch bass on the lake they are fishing. We all enjoy these bits of helpful information, since we are not allowed to get information from noncompetitors. It takes a good friend to share information with someone he or she is competing against.

> **TIP**
>
> If you find schools of bass twenty feet deep and deeper, use a jigging spoon.

God is an even better friend—and He is willing to share more than we can ever imagine. The moment we repent of our sins and ask Him to be our Lord and Savior, God gives us His own Spirit. The Holy Spirit is there to give us answers in any situation. He guides us into what to say and do and gives us wisdom, understanding, discernment, and strength when we need it most. God's Holy Spirit is God's great gift to us!

## JANUARY 5

### MARK 1:40

*Now a leper came to Him, imploring Him, kneeling down to Him and saying to Him, "If You are willing, You can make me clean."*

We all have our favorite lure. Many would say a sinking worm, shaky head, or an even smaller rig, a drop shot. For me, it would be a spinnerbait. I might not catch quite as many, but the pure excitement and teeth-jarring strike makes it my favorite—my confidence bait.

The man with leprosy in today's verse had all confidence in Jesus and in His ability to heal him. He showed that and humbled himself by kneeling down. Jesus' answer was that teeth-shattering strike: "I am willing; be cleansed," and the leper was (v. 41). Jesus died on the cross to cleanse us of every sin we have ever committed. We need faith to believe Jesus is the Son of God and has the power to forgive us. We need to humble ourselves, repent of our sins, and ask Jesus to save us—and He will.

**TIP**

When the water is super cold, try the old twin spin on steep banks.

JIMMY HOUSTON

JOSHUA 21:45

*Not a word failed of any good thing which the L*ORD
*had spoken to . . . Israel. All came to pass.*

I love it when a plan comes together. We all do! We all dream and plan for that great fishing trip, a huge personal best bass, the perfect memory with our family. Often it happens; sometimes it doesn't.

Has God put a good thing in your mind and on your heart? Has it come to pass? I believe it will. Not all of what we want to happen comes from God. Much of it is simply our own wants. But God places dreams, goals, and promises inside us through His Holy Spirit. God is working today to make those come to pass. He is setting up the right people, the right situation, and the right time to make it happen. We need to do our part. We need to honor God in all we do until that good thing comes to pass.

**TIP**
A lipless crankbait or rattlebait works great in cold water above grass.

JOHN 15:16

*"You did not choose Me, but I chose you and appointed you that you should go and bear fruit."*

One of the great things about fishing is you get to pick who you play with. You can fish with your wife, husband, kids, girlfriend, or your best buddy. You choose your fishing partners.

Isn't it awesome God chose you and me to be His? The God who created the moon and stars chose us. What if Roland Martin or Hank Parker chose you to be his fishing partner? Well, this is much better than that. This is God! We pick our fishing partners to have fun and catch fish!

By the way, this scripture is Jesus talking. Do you see the last part of the verse: "that you should go and bear much fruit"? God chooses us to bear fruit. That fruit includes joy, peace, and love. What fruit can you and I bear today?

**TIP**
Huge bass suspend over the top of schools of shad in the winter.

2 CHRONICLES 27:6
*Jotham became mighty, because he prepared
his ways before the LORD his God.*

Young tournament fishermen coming out of college
and high school today are amazingly talented. Some
will be successful tournament fishermen; most will not.
Making a living fishing is still a difficult game to play.

Jotham became king when he was
twenty-five, and his dad, Uzziah, when he
was sixteen. Both were young, but both
became mighty and prosperous and reigned
as king nearly seventy years combined.
When you add in Jotham's grandfather and
great-grandfather, they reigned 137 years.
All became king from ages seven to twenty-
five. All became successful; all were in the same family;
all followed God. Whether you come from a Christian
family or not, you can be the one to start a great family
tradition. Prepare your ways, every day, before the Lord
and you will not only become mighty; you just might be
preparing the way to success for generations.

**TIP**
Place old
Christmas
trees around
docks for bass
and crappie.

PROVERBS 5:21

*The ways of man are before the eyes of the*
*Lord, and He ponders all his paths.*

The new fish locators that we fish with today are amazing. They are eyes under the water. We see structure and fish better than ever. We have learned how to identify species and size. We even watch the fish strike our bait.

Today's scripture tells us that God sees our ways. He knows everything we are doing, everything we speak, even what we are thinking. He knows our hearts. It's amazing that God has the power to immediately punish us for our mess-ups and sin, but He doesn't. This scripture tells us He ponders our paths. This means that in God's mercy, He is giving us time to repent and come to Him and be saved. His mercy is waiting on you right now to cover and forgive your sins.

**TIP**
Heated fishing docks are a great place to beat these cold winter days.

JOSHUA 24:15

*If it seems evil to you to serve the LORD, choose for yourselves this day whom you will serve. . . . But as for me and my house, we will serve the LORD.*

Fishing is full of choices; we have hundreds of choices to make on every fishing trip. We make decisions every cast. These decisions aren't life-and-death, but they are important for success and extremely important for tournament fishermen.

In our house, we have today's scripture on a plaque beneath our television. Everyone who looks at that television sees that scripture. Focus on the first line: "If it seems evil to you to serve the LORD." Unfortunately, right here in America and around the world, millions believe it *is* evil to serve the Lord! It is time for those of us who do serve Him to stand up and proclaim who we serve. Serving the Lord has more advantages in your life, your family, your finances, your health, your career, everything, than serving anything else. *It's your choice.*

**TIP**

Paddlefish congregate in rivers during winter and can be found with today's fish locators.

ACTS 4:33

*With great power the apostles gave witness to the resurrection of the Lord Jesus. And great grace was upon them all.*

I do around a hundred personal appearances a year. These include boat shows, churches, trade shows, conventions, and motivational speaking. I visit with thousands of folks at these events every year. They come to talk with me and listen to my views on whatever subject and venue I may be working. And it's all in person.

The early spread of the gospel of Jesus Christ was all done in person too. There were no television ads, no social media, no email blitzes, and thankfully no robocalls. Do you think the gospel would have ever evangelized the world if God wasn't making it happen? Of course not. The reward new believers received here on earth was great grace. This was favor from God, and it is the same great grace available to you and me. It might be good to tell someone about Jesus today!

**TIP**

The Disney World lakes have great guided fishing trips available.

2 CHRONICLES 26:5

*He sought God in the days of Zechariah . . . and as long*
*as he sought the LORD, God made him prosper.*

Everyone who fishes seeks help on most fishing trips.
We check the lake report and fishing reports, and if we
know a friend who has fished the lake or lives there, we
give him or her a call to see what's happening. We want to
make that fishing trip a good one.

How much more important is it to seek
God in everything we do and seek Him
daily? Today's verse about God making
a man prosper is about Uzziah, who became
king of Judah at sixteen and reigned fifty-
two years. When we think of prospering, we
usually think only about money. How about
God making us prosper in health, in our
families, our relationships, our church, our
peace, our joy, and much more? I think most
of us want to prosper—and when we seek
God in all we do, we will.

**TIP**
Use square-bill
crankbaits that
won't contact
the bottom for
smallmouth
bass.

MATTHEW 24:30

*"They will see the Son of Man coming on the clouds
of heaven with power and great glory."*

One cool thing about tournament fishing is making it back to the weigh-in on time and having your spouse waiting. I was so nervous on tournament days when my wife, Chris, was fishing her Bass 'n Gal tournaments, watching for her boat to make it in on time to the weigh-in area. She always cut it to under a minute from being late.

Jesus is coming back to earth, and He is coming back right on time at a time decided by God alone—He will not be one second late. Many believe the signs are here and the second coming of Jesus could happen anytime. It would be difficult to debate that stand. What I do know is I am ready, and it will be as sudden as the blink of an eye (1 Corinthians 15:52). Are you ready?

**TIP**

If you tournament fish, make sure you have a good spot very close to the weigh-in area.

PROVERBS 15:8

*The prayer of the upright is His delight.*

It is easy to talk about prayer in tournament fishing. I'll be the first to admit I've said a bazillion prayers in tournament competitions—before, during, and after. Some say they never pray for fish. Yeah, right.

For most of us, prayer is really important, and we pray a lot. But how important is it to God? From an upright person, it is His delight. God loves to hear the prayer of those who belong to Him. We become righteous by the blood of Jesus. We are upright before God by the way we live. On those days when you do and say things that honor Him, that is a perfect time to pray. He will delight in your prayer; and that is when God's favor comes crashing through. God's blessings will rain down. Give it a shot. Live this day uprightly and pray to God, thanking Him for today. See what happens!

**TIP**
To set the hook on a swim jig, simply wind faster.

# JANUARY 15

## JOSHUA 24:29

*Now it came to pass . . . that Joshua . . . the servant of the*
*LORD, died, being one hundred and ten years old.*

God told me I would live to be ninety-five—not quite 110, like Joshua, but still a long life. I didn't hear God's voice from heaven but from inside my heart, spoken to me by God's Holy Spirit.

When the dam broke and we lost our lake here at Twin Eagle Ranch in Oklahoma in 2015, I stood on the bank and cried. It was like being stabbed in the heart by a dagger. It hurt that much. We had enjoyed this lake for twelve years and caught so many fish.

**TIP**
Fish bluff banks in winter.

God brought to my mind the scripture that says God will pay you back double for your loss. He told me I would enjoy this lake again twice that long. Twenty-four more years—to age ninety-five! I think then I will be like Hezekiah and ask God for fifteen more. If God is willing, that's 110 years, same as Joshua. When you have bad things happen, trust God to always make it right.

MATTHEW 6:6

*"But you, when you pray, go into your room, and when you have*
*shut your door, pray to your Father who is in the secret place;*
*and your Father who sees in secret will reward you openly."*

Most everyone who loves to fish has secret fishing holes—places that always seem to have fish. And you need to be a pretty special friend to even be invited to share these secret places. I've had places on Lake Tenkiller so secret that I wouldn't even fish if there was another boat in sight. We simply will not share these secret spots!

**TIP**
Throw a crankbait on a falling tide.

What Jesus was saying to His disciples in today's scripture about praying in a secret place is to not make a big showy deal about your praying. No long, flowery, wordy prayers that are meant to impress those listening. Jesus asked that we pray in secret and talk to God in private, as a friend. The amazing thing is that God rewards those prayers out where all can see. It's our choice: we can pray to be praised by man or pray to be blessed by God.

JOHN 14:26

*"The Helper, the Holy Spirit, whom the Father will
send in My name, He will teach you all things."*

How would you like a free lesson from Kevin VanDam, Roland Martin, or my wife, Chris, to teach you all things about bass fishing? These three have a combined twenty-three B.A.S.S. and Bass 'n Gal Angler of the Year titles. That's right—twenty-three! And I don't even know how many tournament wins.

> **TIP**
>
> Mark a waypoint on your locator on any deep-water structure.

Today's scripture, spoken by Jesus Himself, offers each of us something better. It offers us God's Spirit. We receive this as a free gift from God the moment we are saved. Jesus called God's Holy Spirit the Helper. The key is how much and how often we are allowing God's Spirit to help us. We are often offered help by others that we don't accept for some reason, such as pride, lack of time, obligation, or sometimes even hate. Pay close attention to what God's Holy Spirit is saying to you today. He's trying to help.

LUKE 18:14

*"I tell you . . . everyone who exalts himself will be humbled,*
*and he who humbles himself will be exalted."*

F ishing is like baseball; it is an extremely humbling
sport. Many at the top level of tournament fishing
are almost afraid to brag. I know I am
because it is almost a kiss of death in
tournament fishing.

The Bible implores us to be humble. In
today's scripture, Jesus was talking about
a sinful tax collector who was justified by
humbling himself before God. We humble
ourselves by how we speak and act but
mostly by who or what we put our trust in.
Are we placing ourselves before God? How
about our money, our jobs, our fame, or our
accomplishments? God is a jealous God. He
allows no other but exalts those who put
Him first. When God exalts, we live in His
favor, His blessing, His protection. I like
that deal!

**TIP**

Before fishing
deep structures,
it is best to see
the fish; and
with today's
electronics
(fish finders
and Aqua-Vu
cameras) we can!

EPHESIANS 6:12

*We do not wrestle against flesh and blood, but against principalities, against powers, against the rulers of the darkness of this age, against spiritual hosts of wickedness.*

Some fishing trips are spectacular, almost all are good, but some seem doomed from the start. We forget something important, we have a flat, the boat ramp is closed, a motor breaks down, or the weather turns horrible. One bad thing seems to lead to another, as if we are living under a dark cloud. Well, we are.

Since man's fall, we have been living in an evil world. At no other time in my life have we seen so much wickedness, and that wickedness permeates all segments of our land. Evil spiritual powers have taken control of some of America's most important institutions and companies. How do we fight that and still succeed with joy, peace, and prosperity? By living in truth, righteousness, and faith. The devil's demons don't really stand a chance. Let's rumble!

**TIP**
Follow the birds to locate schools of flickering shad.

1 JOHN 5:4

*Whatever is born of God overcomes the world. And this is the victory that has overcome the world—our faith.*

No tournament victory is ever easy. As many fish as you have found, and as easy as it may look to others, winning is actually next to impossible. It takes overcoming much to win.

When we are saved, born again of God, we immediately become overcomers, conquerors, winners. As saved, born-again believers, we are made for overwhelming success. We have the power to overcome setbacks, bad breaks, enemies, illness, and any other obstacle the devil places in our paths. We will overcome even death, just as Jesus did when He walked out of that grave. Our victory is in our faith, and it need not waver in any situation. Whatever may be in front of you today, whatever the world throws at you, remember you are an overcomer and will have victory.

**TIP**

No matter how cold it gets, there will always be a few bass shallow.

1 PETER 4:16

*If anyone suffers as a Christian, let him not be
ashamed, but let him glorify God in this matter.*

We all have bad days fishing when we just can't catch
fish. Generally there are several reasons we are suffering through not catching much, but usually, it is our
own fault. But what about suffering and being persecuted
when we are doing things right? How do we handle that?

Here in America and around the world, Christians
are being persecuted. The church is under attack. God
said what we need to do is glorify Him and
not be ashamed. We need to stand tall
and feel proud that we are worthy to be
called Christians, chosen by the God who
hung the moon and stars. We are blessed
that we have the Spirit of God in us. As
Christians, we should expect persecution,
we should rejoice in it, we should evaluate
it, and we should entrust it to God. We
will be triumphant.

**TIP**
Practicing
good balance is
essential in bass
fishing. Stay
on your toes!

MARK 8:38

*"Whoever is ashamed of Me and My words in this adulterous and sinful generation, of him the Son of Man also will be ashamed when He comes in the glory of His Father with the holy angels."*

We get hundreds of pictures with fish posted on our Facebook fan page. Many, if not most, are pictures of kids holding or kissing a fish. Plain and simple, we are really proud of our kids and grandkids. And we certainly should be. I sure am!

Jesus was talking about just the opposite here. He was talking about someone being ashamed of Him and His teaching. How could we ever have any hope if Jesus were ashamed of us? We would have none. Praise God, for those of us who are saved and made holy by the blood of Christ, we will never be ashamed of Jesus—and He will never be ashamed of us.

**TIP**

Fish jigs slower during winter months.

PSALM 91:11

*He shall give His angels charge over you to keep you in all your ways.*

My friend Apache, who works and lives here on Twin Eagle Ranch, once had a chain come off his chain saw. When he turned the saw off, he heard a rattlesnake. It was coiled by the tree he was about to cut. It most certainly would have bitten him. He has had several near-disaster accidents working here at the Eagle but has never been hurt. He told me we have angels living here. I believe that too!

**TIP**
Use a 7'3" casting rod for longer wintertime casts.

When we become believers, God dispatches legions of angels to protect us and our loved ones. Angels keep watch over us in our homes, in our vehicles, and on our boats. They go with our kids and grandkids to ball games, dates, and parties. Every Christian has stories where God's angels stepped in and saved the day. Be protected by legions of angels today by trusting Jesus and making Him your Lord and Savior.

PROVERBS 16:3
*Commit your works to the LORD, and your
thoughts will be established.*

E very tournament fisherman has those days where
he or she commits the day (or huge chunks of it)
to one little area or to one lure or one pattern. This
approach can be both good and bad.                    It
generally brings much success or dismal
failure. Not much in between.

Today's proverb tells us to totally commit whatever we are doing or thinking to
God, holding nothing back. When we do
this (and we simply do it by praying), God
causes our thoughts to line up with His
will. Isn't that something amazing? A simple
prayer allows God to guide our thinking.
I'm in on that deal. When our thoughts line
up with God's will, our works and plans will succeed.
Whatever your day holds, whatever your works or plans
are for today, commit them right now to God—and get
ready for more success!

**TIP**
It is best to
store heavy
gear in the back
of your boat.

# JANUARY 25

REVELATION 20:15

*Anyone not found written in the Book of*
*Life was cast into the lake of fire.*

The year 2020 was the first year in fifty-five years that I didn't fish national B.A.S.S. Tournaments. Amazingly, I did not miss the tournaments much, and sometimes didn't even know when one was going on. When I did, I would always look at the list of standings and see how all my buddies were doing, good or bad.

Without a doubt, the most important list we will ever be on is the list of names written in the Book of Life. We will all stand before an almighty God and be judged by our works. We need not win by being the best Christians; we don't even have to be near the top; we just have to be in the book. Our names are placed in that Book of Life the moment we are saved and make Jesus our Lord and Savior.

**TIP**

Lightweight shaky head jigs with small worms work well in winter.

HEBREWS 4:16

*Let us therefore come boldly to the throne of grace, that we may obtain mercy and find grace to help in time of need.*

One of the best places to catch fish just about any time of the year or in any weather is below a dam. America has so many man-made lakes with huge dams. There are always lots of fish below these dams because of currents. The more current, usually, the more the fish are biting. These currents are scary and can be dangerous. It does scare me to see folks out there in small jon boats. I am confident fishing these dangerous areas because of my extremely safe twenty-one-foot Ranger boat.

We can be confident, too, to come to an almighty God because of the blood of Jesus. We belong to Him. This allows us to obtain mercy and grace exactly when we need it the most. This perfectly timed grace will help us and take care of everything we need.

**TIP**
Big bass will be shallow under heavy vegetation during winter months.

PSALM 26:11

*As for me, I will walk in my integrity;*
*redeem me and be merciful to me.*

Tournament fishing is an extremely honest sport. Hardly ever does a tournament fisherman break a rule, almost never intentionally. Fishermen in general follow the fishing laws closely. I have fished with hundreds of other fishermen and have seen very few fishing laws or rules broken. Folks who fish tend to have integrity.

In today's scripture, David was setting a really high bar for himself when he told a God who sees and knows everything, "I will walk in my integrity." How could David do that? It was only possible because his heart was tuned in to God's heart. What was he asking God in return for his right living? David was hoping that God would show him mercy and grace and redeem him. Jesus has redeemed us by His blood. We have God's mercy and grace. Our goal every single day should be to walk with God in integrity.

**TIP**

Search out channel swings in the winter.

PHILIPPIANS 1:6

*He who has begun a good work in you will
complete it until the day of Jesus Christ.*

A lmost everyone who fishes, including me, has the goal
to become a better fisherman. We all want to catch
more fish because that is the fun part of this sport. We
buy new lures, learn to use the latest electronics, attend
seminars, watch television shows and videos, and ask
questions.

Paul wrote today's verse from prison
in Rome, but he was still encouraging—
and he shared a universal hope that all
Christians should possess. God has started
a good work in each of us that will come to
fruition. Has God placed a dream or goal in
your heart? A good work that will not only
benefit you but help those around you as
well? Paul said that God will complete that
work: He is working behind the scenes every
day, perfecting that work and dream in you.
Honor God in all you do. Your good work
will come to full completion.

**TIP**
Fish a
crankbait
in creek
channels
leading to
spawning
beds.

JOSHUA 10:12–13

*Joshua spoke to the LORD . . . and he said in the sight
of Israel: "Sun, stand still over Gibeon; and Moon,
in the Valley of Aijalon." So the sun stood still.*

Stopping time has been a wish of mine forever. Every
fisherman would like for the first hour of daylight or
the last hour before dark to last and last. Every tournament fisherman has longed for just another hour or two
before weigh-in. But I have never prayed for it.

In today's scripture, Joshua prayed,
and he did it right in front of
everyone. His faith was on full
display. Plus, while he was at it, he asked
the moon to stand still as well. And it
did! Not really a big deal for the God who
created it. Do you have a dream or something you want to accomplish? How about
standing like Joshua and asking God to
make that happen? Pray that bold prayer
with utmost faith and confidence. God
just might make it happen.

**TIP**

Rip a crankbait
through grass
to create
strikes.

GENESIS 22:8

*Abraham said, "My son, My God will provide for*
*Himself the lamb for a burnt offering."*

One of the statements we hear a lot from folks we fish with is, "Don't worry; I have an ace in the hole!" That usually happens after a few hours without much success. We tell people, "If you have an ace in the hole, let's go fish that first."

Abraham had an ace in the hole: his God and his belief in that God. Asked to sacrifice his son, he obeyed. When his son Isaac asked, "Where is the lamb to be sacrificed?" Abraham spoke the famous words in today's verse. A critical point is that Isaac, who was around twenty-five, agreed with his father that God would provide. He allowed Abraham, his very old father, to tie him up and place him on the wood to be sacrificed. And God did come through with a ram for sacrifice instead of Isaac. Whatever you are believing for, God has the power to provide.

**TIP**

Often a sweep and pause with your rod will trigger crankbait strikes.

HEBREWS 11:6

*Without faith it is impossible to please Him, for he who comes to God must believe that He is, and that He is a rewarder of those who diligently seek Him.*

Tournament practice is three days of extreme searching for places and patterns to catch fish during the competition. We diligently look for the best places so we can do well in the tournament.

Today's scripture contains simple instruction from God. We are rewarded for diligently seeking Him. How do we do this? Through faith. By believing that God is the real and only God. Having full confidence that God can reward us with righteousness and forgiveness. Most people believe that God exists; but that is not the whole deal. Faith is real belief that God spoke the world into existence— real belief that Jesus walked on water, made blind people see, raised the dead, fed thousands with a couple of fish, and rose from the grave. And it's real belief that He will raise us to be with Him for eternity.

**TIP**
Crankbaits produce well as long as water temperatures stay above 40 degrees Fahrenheit.

FEBRUARY

1 THESSALONIANS 4:16

*The Lord Himself will descend from heaven with a shout, with the voice of an archangel, and with the trumpet of God.*

We used to start bass tournaments with a shotgun blast—and was it ever exciting. When that gun went off, 150–200 boats or more went roaring off in every direction. Boats swamped and ran together, and sometimes throttles were shoved down so hard they broke off. It was crazy!

Today's scripture is about a shout heard around the world by billions. That shout will bring fear and trembling to all, but that will be quickly replaced by wonderful joy for those of us caught up in the clouds to meet Jesus. Think about that: hundreds of thousands, perhaps millions of born-again Christians leaving this earth to be with God forever in heaven! We don't know the time or the date. Imagine the scene when He comes back to earth with a shout. Are you ready?

**TIP**
The biggest mistake made in the winter is fishing too fast—slow down!

JOHN 16:22

*"I will see you again and your heart will rejoice,
and your joy no one will take from you."*

My wife and I love it when our kids and grandkids come to Twin Eagle Ranch. When they drive up, we are so eager to see them that we rush out and meet them in the circle drive. During the coronavirus, many older folks stayed away from family for long periods of time due to health concerns. Imagine that immense joy when they could finally see them again.

In today's verse, Jesus was talking to His closest disciples right before He was betrayed by Judas, arrested, beaten, humiliated, and killed on the cross. He encouraged them and assured them that their sorrow would turn into joy, and it did after Jesus walked out of that grave! Whatever your situation in life is today, Jesus can give you joy that is permanent. Ask in His name for that joy today.

**TIP**
Fish a steep bank more thoroughly in cold water.

PSALM 37:25
*I have been young, and now am old; yet I*
*have not seen the righteous forsaken.*

Becoming a better fisherman takes commitment: a commitment of time, money, effort, and skills to become better. This kind of commitment is rare in youngsters but extremely important to us all if we are going to become what God wants us to be in life.

Righteous living requires commitment to God, sure, but even more difficult is commitment to oneself not to compromise on ethics. It's easy in this day of free-wheeling and dealing to compromise our righteousness. *Just a little compromise will be okay to make this deal work. Just a little white lie won't hurt in this circumstance.* On top of that, what used to be wrong is now okay in the eyes of the world, but remember it is still wrong. Righteousness comes with a great reward: God will not forsake you—ever! Live a righteous life today and know that God is with you every step of the way.

**TIP**
Rocks and hard bottoms become important in cold water because they hold heat and baitfish.

EPHESIANS 3:20

*[He] is able to do exceedingly abundantly above all that we ask or think, according to the power that works in us.*

We all dream big in fishing! These days on YouTube and Facebook, it's a big deal to share our personal best. If you happen to be involved in tournament fishing, you definitely have all kinds of dreams, goals, and ambitions.

TIP

Fish small, deep, sunshiny pockets on clear, cold lakes.

Today's verse makes those dreams come true. God's power that He places in us allows us to accomplish things beyond our wildest imagination. Hang your hat on this one. The power that He has put in you and me is pretty much unlimited. Think big; ask big; pray big; expect big things to happen! Be sure today that you are totally devoted to God. Include Him in everything you do. And when you do, you will have all of God's power, majesty, wisdom, goodness, love, and patience working in you. Expect abundance; expect God's greatness.

PROVERBS 3:5

*Trust in the LORD with all your heart, and*
*lean not on your own understanding.*

Wintertime fishing is probably the most dangerous fishing we can do. It takes quite a bit of trust to crawl in a boat and go ten to twenty miles or more out on the water to go fishing, knowing that the air temperature or water temperature alone could kill you. Trust in your equipment, your skills, and, yep, trust in your God. I have come close to being killed several times. Most were because I was violating today's proverb and leaning on my own understanding.

I think what God is asking in today's verse is all about involvement. Our God wants to be included in all we do. He does that when we allow Him completely into our hearts. Once our hearts come under the will of God, we begin making better decisions based on God's will, not our own understanding. Let God come fully into your heart today and watch what happens.

**TIP**

Learn to identify bass and crappie from other species on your locator.

EXODUS 20:12

*Honor your father and your mother, that your*
*days may be long upon the land.*

F ishing is by nature a family sport. Anyone at any age
can enjoy fishing. My best memories are fishing with
my mom and dad, my granddad, and my uncles. We
have passed that on by fishing with our
kids, grandkids, nieces, and great-
grandkids. I know every fishing
family has made these lasting memories.

**TIP**
Most winter
fish are located
on or near the
main lake.

Today's verse about family is found in
the middle of the Ten Commandments God
gave Moses. It seems totally out of place
to me on the list and is numbered before
commands against some dastardly sins, such
as murder, adultery, stealing, lying, and coveting. What I see is how important family is
to God. It's so important He placed family on a pedestal
for all mankind forever. This commandment is so important for us that God gave it with a blessing: long life. It
might be the perfect day to give your mom and dad a call
if they are still here with us.

MARK 11:25

*"Whenever you stand praying, if you have anything against anyone, forgive him, that your Father in heaven may also forgive you your trespasses."*

Forgiveness is a big part of fishing. Even our fishing line is made with forgiveness built in. It's called stretch, and it allows fishing line to give just the right amount and not break. Without this forgiveness in our fishing line, we would lose many big fish.

**TIP**

Follow deep balls of bait to find schools of fish.

Today's scripture is a hard one for most of us. Jesus had just told Peter that whatever he prayed for, believe that he had it and he would have it. That is good, but then Jesus added this: He said to forgive anyone, meaning friends, enemies, believers, nonbelievers, whoever. It also includes forgiving them for everything, whether minor disagreements or major sins. He had told Peter that to have successful prayer, you need faith. But then He added that to have success we must forgive anyone for anything. Isn't that what God does for us?

ROMANS 8:28

*All things work together for good to those who love God,*
*to those who are called according to His purpose.*

The middle of February is the time here in the South when we start to turn the corner from winter to spring. Sure, there is plenty of cold weather to come, but we start having warmer days, the cold fronts are shorter, and the wind blows more from the south. All these things, working together, improve fishing.

Today's verse is the primary one I rely on for strong faith and belief in my Savior. First, it is awesome that God called us, you and me. Next, it means anything good, bad, horrible, or fantastic will work together for my good. What seems terrible, even catastrophic, will work for my good. I have had circumstances that felt like a kick in the gut, that brought me to my knees, that still worked out supernaturally for my good. Lean on this; it works!

**TIP**

Fish seem to bite best on low tide.

TITUS 3:5

*Not by works of righteousness which we have done,*
*but according to His mercy He saved us.*

W hen we have something wonderful just fall into our laps, we get excited and feel blessed. We did not work for it, did not deserve it, but we got it anyway. We backlash, pick out the backlash, and there is a fish on it. Our lure hangs in a tree, and a fish bites it. My buddy Scott Canterbury, 2019 B.A.S.S. Angler of the Year, was retying a leader during a tournament and dragging a drop shot behind the boat when he caught the big fish of the tournament. It was a huge happening, but it's nothing compared to God's mercy when He saves us!

Nothing we have done has earned us salvation. It is God's gift from His mercy—from His love, from His grace. All Scott had to do was reel that fish in. All we need to do is accept God's mercy.

**TIP**

Wintertime fish are more active under low pressure and cloud cover.

LUKE 1:47

*"My spirit has rejoiced in God my Savior."*

Sure, it's fun to win, but some of my happiest times tournament fishing were turning really bad tournaments or tournament days into successes, coming back from bad days to make great ones, figuring out the situations that moved the ordinary to the extraordinary. These days brought joy and made super memories.

Today's verse was spoken by Mary, the mother of Jesus, after she had traveled to visit Elizabeth, the mother of John the Baptist. Mary was filled with joy and happiness knowing she had been chosen by God to give birth to Jesus but also knowing that God was her Savior. She still needed God's grace for salvation. She was praying to God about her lowly state in life being changed by God's mercy so that she would be called blessed forever. Isn't that what God is offering us as well? The opportunity to rejoice in God and be blessed forever?

**TIP**
Try suspended jerkbaits on sunny winter days in clear water.

1 SAMUEL 2:30

*But now the L*ORD *says . . . "For those who honor Me I will honor, and those who despise Me shall be lightly esteemed."*

F ishing competition produces winners and champions. All types of competition do, and with that comes awards and honors. When we compete, honor is not our goal; our goal is to catch fish and have fun—but when we are honored, it feels pretty good.

I have always said we should try to honor God in all we do to have success. But think about what today's verse says: God will honor us. Wow. I cannot think of anyone I would rather be honored by than the God who hung the moon and stars. The rest of this verse is even more remarkable. I have never despised God. It is amazing that even the ones who do despise God are not despised by Him; they are "lightly esteemed." This shows God's love and mercy and His goodness to mankind. Honor God today, and watch Him honor your life!

**TIP**

Runoff from warm rains can warm water up quickly. Do not overlook these runoffs—even in dirty water.

1 PETER 5:7

*[Cast] all your cares upon Him, for He cares for you.*

We tell friends who visit Twin Eagle Ranch that we have a box at the front gate, and we recommend that they put their worries in that box when they come through the gate! No cares, no worries at Twin Eagle. Just have a fantastic time. For most, it works; it is hard to be at the Eagle and worry.

God is a little like that box; He is asking for our cares, big or small. How good is a day without cares? How great is a worry-free week? How about living our lives care-free? This is about trust. Before we can live carefree, we must trust God to handle those cares—really cast our worries on Him. Can we do that all the time? Do I? No, not really; but I am getting better at it. The best thing is, when I do, God comes through every time.

**TIP**
Clay banks hold spotted bass all year long.

DANIEL 3:1

*Nebuchadnezzar the king made an image of gold, whose*
*height was sixty cubits and its width six cubits.*

ishing is important to a lot of us. It is more than a
hobby, more than a sport, more than friendly competition. It is a way of life. Can fishing become our God?
I think it can. There might be a thin line
between fishing becoming our
God and not, particularly for those
who fish for a living. But God allows no
other God. He doesn't share His throne.

TIP
Fish shallow
cover near
deep water.

In today's verse we find a blatant example
of a man declaring himself as god. The king
created a ninety-foot-tall statue that all were
commanded to bow down and worship. But
the gods in our lives will not necessarily be
that obvious. They can slip in little by little
until they are on the throne. These gods can take many
forms: a hobby, a job, a sport, money, power, sex. Who or
what are we really worshiping? Is God on your throne?

2 TIMOTHY 1:7

*God has not given us a spirit of fear, but of*
*power and of love and of a sound mind.*

Tournament fishermen are pretty much bulletproof.
We throw caution to the wind and go miles and miles
under any type of situation just to try to catch a good
string of fish. If you are prone to fear, tournaments are
not for you. Fear is a bad thing, not a good thing, and
definitely not a God thing.

Fear comes from the devil. He will
do all he can to put fear in your mind
and heart. God has given us a spirit of power
to overcome fear, a spirit of love. We know
that God loves us so much that He holds
us tight through the scariest of life's storms.
A sound mind and godly wisdom give us
answers to the most frightening questions.
*Fear not*; live today by that. Live your life
by that!

**TIP**
Use heavier
scrounger
jigs dressed
with a Luck-E-
Swim bait for
deep water.

PROVERBS 24:4
*By knowledge the rooms are filled with all*
*precious and pleasant riches.*

Folks walk into our boat building and are amazed at the amount of fishing tackle we have. It is a lot, and yet we still get more when we need it. Chris calls it sinful to have that much tackle. I think it is a building filled with precious and pleasant riches!

Whatever knowledge, whatever skills, whatever athletic abilities I have came from God. Without God blessing me with knowledge and wisdom from Him, I probably wouldn't even need a place for fishing tackle. The wisdom and understanding of God is the blueprint for building a happy home, a loving family, and a successful and full life—one loaded with blessings. God wants all of the above for you and me. He is eager to bless us with His wisdom, understanding, and knowledge. Call on Him today.

**TIP**

Near a dam is a good place to start looking for winter bass. Concentrate on rocks with the sun shining on them.

1 THESSALONIANS 5:16–17
*Rejoice always, pray without ceasing.*

**W**intertime fishing can be brutal. But a real fisherman goes no matter what, and he or she will have a good time regardless of the weather or whether the fish are biting.

Today's verse captures one of many times Paul told Christians to continually be happy, always have a smile on your face, always enjoy life. He wrote most of these encouraging words from prison. Should we really live our lives this way, rejoicing always? Absolutely! How can we do this when life throws so much bad at us? We do it by praying thankful prayers continually—thanking God, thanking God, thanking God! We pray a prayer that perseveres through bad circumstances. We do it with a glad heart that refuses to have a pity party. Paul was in prison, but he knew he had victory in Christ. Rejoice! You and I have that same victory.

> **TIP**
> Dip the tips of soft plastic crawfish in chartreuse Spike-It Dip-N-Glo to add both color and scent.

LUKE 1:46

*Mary said: "My soul magnifies the Lord."*

Fishermen have long joked that the people who catch the biggest fish are the ones who have the longest arms—holding a fish way out and very close to the camera. I am told that some of the new GoPro cameras have a fish-eye lens that really make a fish look huge.

What Mary, the mother of Jesus, did as she began her short but very thankful prayer to God was to magnify God with everything she had. She was filled with joy and thankfulness that God had chosen her to be the mother of the Savior of the world. Should our prayers be a little more like Mary's? Should our souls, our lives, our words, our everyday activities magnify our God? I think they should. I believe the more we do that, the more God will magnify us. Try it and see.

**TIP**

Floating tire reefs are excellent bass cover. You can find these around marinas. Bass suspend under these reefs.

MARK 16:15

*He said to them, "Go into all the world and preach the gospel to every creature."*

Confidence is the best lure in your tackle box. Believe that you are in the right spot at the right time, that you're fishing the best bait to catch fish, and that you are going to get a bite on the very next cast. This is confidence.

Do you have the confidence to believe that Jesus died on the cross to pay for our sins and walked out of the grave three days later to give us victory over death? Our part is to believe and to repent of our sins and ask Jesus to come into our hearts and save us. Make Him Lord of your life and He will. Have you done that? If you haven't, do that right now. If you have, go tell someone. After all, this command is from the One who hung on the cross and walked out of that grave— Jesus Christ Himself.

> **TIP**
> Texas rigged craws work great in grass—even in cold water.

PSALM 34:1

*I will bless the LORD at all times; His praise*
*shall continually be in my mouth.*

Fishermen love to talk about their stuff—how fast
their boat is or how they use only the finest rods and
reels. Their baits are the best, their
fishing line, sunglasses, outboard
engine, electronics, just about anything
they use. We heap praise on a lot of stuff
we own. Hey, I am just as guilty as the
next guy.

How much are we praising what we
really should be praising? The God who
created us, the God who saved us, the
God who sustains us, the God who loves
us—and I could go on forever. David said
in this psalm that we should bless God all the time—
continually praise Him. Today's scripture would be good
for us to tape on the bathroom mirror and the refriger-
ator. When we bless God, He will save us from fear and
deliver us from all our troubles.

> **TIP**
> Heavier jigs
> create more
> noise on
> rocks. This
> attracts bass.

JEREMIAH 29:11

*I know the thoughts that I think toward you, says the LORD, thoughts of peace and not of evil, to give you a future and a hope.*

I love wintertime fishing even though the days are dark and cold, basically gloomy—because crappie fishing can be exceptional, and crappie fishing in a heated, lighted boat dock can make those cold, dark winter days really fun. Most boat docks are baited with trees or structures that make these docks even better.

This letter by Jeremiah in today's scripture was given to the Israelites at their darkest moment. They had been taken away defeated, naked, and ashamed into captivity, exiled to another country for seventy years as prophesied. God promised peace. He promised a future. He promised them hope! These promises remain today for us; at our darkest, most hopeless times, God's thoughts are to give us a hope and a bright future.

TIP

A beaver-type soft plastic bait fishes through thick grass easily.

PSALM 121:2

*My help comes from the LORD, who made heaven and earth.*

Something that helped me most in my early days learning to fish a jig was when my dad told me the bass wouldn't drop the jig very often. I did not have to be perfect; in fact I didn't even need to know exactly when they bit. They still had that jig in their mouth; I could swim the jig or fish it on slack line and not worry about the bass spitting it out. No matter what happened, I could be secure in that knowledge and catch that fish.

It's assuring to go about our days and know that whatever happens, we can be secure in knowing our help comes from the God who spoke today into existence. God doesn't sleep; He's here for us every second of every day. How is that possible? The second you are saved and make Jesus your Lord and Savior, God places His Holy Spirit inside you to provide all the help you will ever need!

**TIP**

Bass move to points near bends of rivers and creek channels early in pre-spawn.

MARK 13:27

*"He will send His angels, and gather together His elect from the four winds, from the farthest part of earth to the farthest part of heaven."*

Tournament anglers often make what they call a "milk run." They have ten or more spots to stop and fish during the day. As the day goes on, they plan on catching a bass or two at several of these stops and end the day with a strong limit.

In today's verse, Jesus was talking about sending His angels on the biggest milk run in all history: picking up His elect, His chosen, His redeemed. Picking up you and me. His tremendous power and glory will be on full display for all mankind to see. We don't know when that day, that milk run, will happen. But Jesus said it will. Many think the signs are here right now. Jesus told us to watch and be ready. I'm ready! Are you ready?

**TIP**
A Mimic Impersonator without a rattle produces well in clear, cold water.

PROVERBS 12:10

*A righteous man regards the life of his animal.*

**M**y buddy Gary Yamamoto always has a practice partner or two during practice days for FLW pro tournaments. It's common knowledge that I stopped fishing national tournaments due to rule changes that didn't allow my wife, Chris, to practice with me. How does Gary get away with having a practice partner? It isn't his wife, Beverly; it's Gary's precious little dogs! Rain or shine, they go fishing with Gary.

God was saying in today's verse that consistently righteous people take care of their animals. Proverbs is full of attributes of the righteous. Righteous folks help their neighbors, tell the truth, are honest, are dependable, work hard, and more! For God to include animals with such merited characteristics shows how much God regards the life He created. I think most of us regard the lives of our animals about the same as members of our family. Pretty sure I do. 'Bout time to feed the animals!

**TIP**
If it is legal, build brush piles on the ice for better fishing later.

JOHN 16:33

*"These things I have spoken to you, that in Me you may have peace. In the world you will have tribulation; but be of good cheer, I have overcome the world."*

One of the worst storms that I've encountered on the water, even to this day, was way back in 1976, the year I won my first B.A.S.S. Angler of the Year title. The storm included high winds, rain, lightning, plus heavy and large hail. Definitely life-threatening. Not only did my God see me through the storm but I won the tournament!

Jesus spoke the words in today's scripture to His closest friends right before He was arrested and crucified. He knew exactly what was about to happen and how His followers would be treated; they would have tribulation. He was also talking to you and me too. He was telling us to take courage, be confident, be happy! Jesus has taken away the power of Satan to harm us. Go out and live today in victory. You serve an awesome and powerful God.

**TIP**
Wearing polarized sunglasses will help your fishing.

2 CORINTHIANS 12:9

*He said to me, "My grace is sufficient for you, for*
*My strength is made perfect in weakness."*

One thing we have between us and the fish is our fishing line. It's only as strong as its weakest spot. A nick or rough spot can turn fifteen-to-twenty-pound test line into half that! That tiny weakness in the line can cost us a fish of a lifetime.

We have weaknesses in our lives, our bodies, our minds. Paul's was physical: he called it a thorn in his flesh (see 2 Corinthians 12:7–10). Paul asked the Lord to remove it three times and was denied. But God gave him grace. God's favor and mercy, love and kindness gave Paul supernatural power and strength to endure.

God's power and strength are on full display in our weaknesses. We will all go through trials and problems in life that we can't handle on our own. God's grace was sufficient to see Paul through it, and God's grace will empower us as well.

**TIP**
Crawfish colors may be the best in late February.

REVELATION 21:4

*God will wipe away every tear from their eyes; there*
*shall be no more death, nor sorrow, nor crying.*

We're all looking for that perfect place to fish, the biggest fish, and the best fishing. We remember near-perfect days, like one I had fishing with Chris at Gibbons Creek Reservoir in Texas. Big fish after big fish! My biggest bass, I caught on Lake Hanabanilla in Cuba, fishing with Chris. My daughter, Sherri's, biggest bass was on Caddo Creek Lake. These are almost perfect days etched into our memories.

**TIP**
This is a perfect time to have your outboard serviced.

God has prepared perfect days for you and me, and not just one every now and then. We'll have perfect days forever! No pain, no tears, no sorrow. I believe we will all be young. Everybody will see; everybody will hear; everybody will walk or run or fly. No more diets, no more wrinkles. No cheating, lying, gossiping, stealing, or killing. No more politics. Sounds like heaven. Well, it is.

PHILIPPIANS 4:13

*I can do all things through Christ who strengthens me.*

Casting accuracy takes practice, especially with a casting reel. Many have problems learning how to use a casting reel, and after a few backlashes they just give up. When I was young, my dad gave me a new casting reel and told me to learn how to use it, or else! I don't know what the "or else" really was, but I was determined to master this new skill. And after about a bazillion backlashes, I did it. I felt strong—as if I could accomplish anything.

**TIP**
Light casting reels like Lew's Titanium Pro T-1 perfectly match Jimmy Houston Blaze Series rods.

Paul was preaching from prison in today's verse and encouraging the church at Philippi about just how powerful Jesus had made him. Jesus had given Paul strength to withstand all things. As a believer, I have that strength. Even when we have nothing, God sustains us until we have what we need. We are very capable of handling anything through God's supernatural strength. He has that strength ready for you right now.

1 SAMUEL 30:6

*David strengthened himself in the LORD.*

In our clearer-water lakes, this is jerkbait season. We mostly want to use a suspended jerkbait—one that stays at the depth we stop it, not one that floats back to the top. Use light line. Although not very strong, and hard to throw on a casting reel, six-pound test line will usually get more bites. It's one of those odd situations where weakness leads to success.

Today's scripture finds David in a perilous situation where he was weak. His own men were threatening to stone him to death. He had returned home to a burned and plundered village. Alone and destitute, David turned to God for strength. He had not consulted God in advance, but now David prayed! He asked God's advice, then followed that advice. This is the key to our success in times of trouble and hardship. Run to God and follow His advice. Be encouraged, and God's Holy Spirit will guide you to success.

**TIP**
Use light solder wire on hooks to turn floating jerkbaits into suspending ones.

MARCH

GENESIS 6:8

*Noah found grace in the eyes of the LORD.*

High water is a bonanza for fishermen. It drives the fish up shallow and makes them easier to catch. One of the absolute best places to find them is people's flooded yards at the banks. Those lawns usually have lots of earthworms pop out of the ground, and fish love them. Flooded yards are also pretty easy to fish. Be extra careful with your boat, though. Don't damage somebody's yard!

Floods may make fishing productive but can be downright deadly for mankind. Noah is the top flood expert ever, and we can all learn from him. Noah was a just and righteous man. Because he was blameless in an evil generation, and he walked with God on a regular basis, God chose Noah and his family to save. Walk with God and honor Him daily, and you will find grace and favor from Him.

> **TIP**
> When the water floods, even if it's cold, throw a white buzzbait.

MARK 10:49

*Then they called the blind man, saying to him,*
*"Be of good cheer. Rise, He is calling you."*

An effective way to fish grass is to find a grass flat and blind cast over it. Depending on how deep the grass is, lipless crankbaits and spinnerbaits work great. Keep scanning with your LiveScope and watch for high spots and low spots in the grass as well as fish moving in and out of the vegetation. It's exciting how that technology allows us to see the unseeable.

In today's scripture, blind Bartimaeus got excited when he heard Jesus coming down the road. He kept crying out, "Jesus, Son of David, have mercy on me!" (v. 47). Can you imagine what he thought when the disciples said, "Rise, He is calling you"? Bartimaeus, though blind, knew Jesus was walking down the road to him, and he received his sight. One bright day, those of us who are saved will hear God say "Rise! He is calling you!" What a day that will be.

**TIP**
The Mimic Impersonator works well over grass and offers perfect depth control.

2 KINGS 6:16

*"Do not fear, for those who are with us are more than those who are with them."*

One thing about bass fishing to remember is, if you catch one, there are usually more close by. Bass are rarely alone. If there are a bunch, it's a honey hole.

If we are saved, we are like those bass. We are never alone. God is always with us. The scripture for today comes from one of my favorite stories about God's presence with us. The prophet Elisha's servant, surrounded by a great army, cried out to Elisha, "What shall we do?" Elisha answered and asked God to open his servant's eyes and let him see. God complied and the servant saw the mountains were full of horses and chariots of fire. God's army surrounded them and was ready to defend them. And it's still there today to fight your battles and mine!

**TIP**
Rubber washers work well for storing umbrella rigs.

PROVERBS 16:24

*Pleasant words are like a honeycomb, sweetness
to the soul and health to the bones.*

Thunder Thornton and Phillip Fulmer, former national
champion coach and athletic director at the University
of Tennessee, fish with me occasionally. On a recent trip
to our ranch, Coach Fulmer brought me two jars of very
special honey. The label simply read, "Coach's Honey."
What a perfect gift from Phillip's per-
sonal honeycombs! Especially for a guy
like me, who loves honey. I even eat a
little bread with it sometimes!

The Bible talks about honey as very
important to our health and well-being. It
gives us energy, brightens our eyes, and even
causes a happy countenance. In today's verse,
God was telling us that saying nice things
gives the same results. You can bring sweetness to your mind and health to your body just by saying
something nice. Imagine how much better the world
would be if we all went out there and did a little doctor-
ing today with pleasant words.

**TIP**
Glue
swimbaits
to your jig
heads.

### JOHN 10:28

*"I give them eternal life, and they shall never perish;*
*neither shall anyone snatch them out of My hand."*

Shad kills (a situation when a significant number of shad die) happen in most man-made lakes during hard winters. This is perfectly normal and will still leave plenty of shad to spawn and replenish the baitfish. Shad kills provide incredible fishing! Shad-colored crankbaits and smaller spinnerbaits work well around the dying shad.

Unlike those shad, we are not doomed to death, but we have been given eternal life. In today's scrip- ture, Jesus was talking to religious Jews who wanted to stone Him. He was talking about His followers, His sheep, to whom He guaranteed eternal life. He was speaking of you and me. Plus, Jesus was warning the devil that no person or thing can take us away from Him. Throughout all eternity, nothing can destroy us—not even death. Jesus has won victory over death, and He has given that life-winning trophy to you and me as well.

**TIP**

When you see a fast-moving bass on your fish finder, that fish is usually ready to bite.

ISAIAH 43:1

*"Fear not, for I have redeemed you; I have called
you by your name; you are Mine."*

Crawfish are called lots of different names. I grew
up calling them crawdads. In Louisiana, they call
them mudbugs. Big bass call them lunch and
dinner! Now is the perfect time to throw
crawfish-colored baits, jigs, cranks,
and spinnerbaits. In most parts of the
country, bass have gone several months
without crawfish. When they see these
crawfish-looking baits—*game on*.

What are we called? According to
today's verse, God calls us His. He calls
us redeemed. Jesus paid a price for our
souls, and we need never fear the devil, his
demons, or anything else this world throws
at us. God calls us personally, individually
to be His. All He asks is that we believe in
His Son, Jesus, and be saved. Ask Jesus to
be Lord of your life. God is calling right now. Will you
answer?

## TIP

A 6'6" to 7'
medium–heavy
or medium
action spinning
rod is perfect
for Ned rigs,
wacky rigs, and
drop shot rigs.

GALATIANS 5:22–23
*The fruit of the Spirit is love, joy, peace, longsuffering, kindness, goodness, faithfulness, gentleness, self-control.*

Can you name nine characteristics or attitudes that would make you a good fisherman? How about a great tournament fisherman? Whatever you come up with, most of us would want these nine qualities.

Take a look at the list in today's scripture that Paul wrote to the Christians in Galatia. How many of these attributes would you put on your list to be a good fisherman? Honestly, I would place all nine of these on mine. Whatever you are trying to become good or great at, these nine attitudes will serve as a solid foundation. How do we get these? We get them from the Holy Spirit, whom God gives us instantly when we make Him our Lord and Savior. From that point on, we're on our way to greatness. Take an inventory and see how you measure up in these nine characteristics.

**TIP**

A shallow square-bill will produce around rocks and wood with water temperatures in the forties on calm sunny days.

1 KINGS 3:13

*"I have also given you what you have not asked: both riches and honor."*

There may not be a fisherman in the world who hasn't prayed while fishing. I would almost bet the ranch that every tournament fisherman has, even the non-Christians! I'll confess right here and now, I've prayed several times every day in every tournament. I wonder how many times we pray a prayer that just really lights God up and excites Him.

Solomon did just that. He asked God for wisdom and understanding to be able to govern and help God's people. God basically answered, "I'll do that, and even more. Riches, honor, a long life." Wow! What an awesome God Solomon served. Yes, sir—He's the same God you and I serve and are praying to today, and He wants to bless us so much. Let's pray something to God today that gets Him excited and see what happens.

**TIP**

Almost always make multiple casts when the water is still cold.

PSALM 37:7

*Rest in the LORD, and wait patiently for Him.*

The key to catching big—really big—alligator gar is using big bait. Sure, we can and do catch them on lures. But to target the huge river monsters, we need a big piece of cut carp. The key is to patiently give alligator gar time to eat the bait. We sometimes follow the gar a hundred to two hundred yards down the river before we set the hook. It takes patience.

King David was telling us here to lean on God and be patient. David himself waited around twenty years or so from the time the prophet Samuel anointed him to be king until he actually became king. If you have a dream, if you have a goal, something you really believe, don't give up on God. Stay in peace; God is working with you, just as He worked with David, until the perfect time came to set the hook. Your time is closer now than ever.

**TIP**

The first dock or two inside a pocket from the main lake is usually the best.

JOHN 21:6

*[Jesus] said to them, "Cast the net on the right side
of the boat, and you will find some [fish]."*

When Chris and I visited Israel a few years back to do
a fishing show (along with our son, Jamie; his wife,
Mandi; friends Joe and Sandi Hall; and Pat Turner, who
runs our production company), we
heard today's scripture over and over.
Chris even quoted it to me several
times. You see, I was extremely unsuccessful
catching fish! I still remember that one (and
only) fish I hooked and lost on the Sea of
Galilee, also called Lake Gennesaret.

Of course, it wasn't which side of the
boat Peter fished—it was Jesus who made
the difference. I can tell you, it is still Jesus
who makes the difference. Whatever your
disappointments, whatever your mess-ups, failures, mis-
treatments, or heartaches, you can trust Jesus to keep you
fishing on the right side of the boat.

**TIP**

In tournaments,
change your
locator trail
colors every day.

PSALM 73:23–24

*You hold me by my right hand. You will guide me with*
*Your counsel, and afterward receive me to glory.*

We all have our favorite baits. It's no secret that mine
is a spinnerbait. My advice has always been to learn
to use all baits well. Pro fishermen get tagged as experts
on certain lures, but let me tell you—these top dawgs are
experts with every bait!

Today's scripture sums up just what an expert God
is and how much He loves you and me.
Wherever we are, whatever we are doing,
God is holding our hands. All the guidance, counsel, wisdom, knowledge,
instruction, and understanding I need
will be mine through God's Holy Spirit,
who is the gift we receive the moment we
believe. And when it's all over here on this
earth and this life ends, eternity begins
with God in His glory. God, He's my
expert and will be forever.

**TIP**

Search for warm
underwater
springs. They
attract large
numbers of
crawfish, bass,
and crappie.

JOSHUA 3:16

*The waters which came down from upstream stood*
*still, and rose in a heap very far away at Adam.*

We all love dead-calm water—water like glass. It gives us a sense of peace. This special time usually comes early in the morning or right before dark. It generally doesn't last long. It's so calm we must exercise stealth to catch fish. We run our trolling motors on low speeds and let baits sit until the ripples die down. It's a magic time.

The events in today's verse were not magic; they were miraculous. Just as the exodus of over a million Jews had begun some forty years earlier, it ended with another display of God's great power. Amazingly, the waters were dammed up miles upstream so the Israelites could cross over the Jordan River to safety. If God can do this, I'm positive He can perform whatever miracles you and I need in our lives.

**TIP**

On grass edges, flip the edge of the grass and about a foot inside the grass edge with jigs and soft plastics.

PSALM 34:7

*The angel of the LORD encamps all around those*
*who fear Him, and delivers them.*

S ome of my earliest memories of figuring out on my
own how to catch fish were on camping trips to Lake
Tenkiller. We lived near Moore, Oklahoma, nearly two
hundred miles away from the lake.
My mom, dad, aunts, and uncles
loved to camp on this lake. I would
get up at daylight before anyone else and
fish the bank around our camp. I caught so
many bass, bluegill, crappie, white bass, and
catfish, and I still fish those same shorelines
from a boat.

Fishing by myself at six or seven years
old all the way to my teenage years, I
certainly must have had angels with me. I
can't remember a single time when I felt any
danger, even though I was often fishing a step away from
thirty feet of water. My angel, and perhaps the one David
was talking about, surely must have been on duty full-
time. I bet yours is too.

**TIP**

Squarebill
crankbaits
with a tight
wobble will
hang up less.

HEBREWS 13:2

*Do not forget to entertain strangers, for by so doing
some have unwittingly entertained angels.*

A key to becoming a good fisherman is to pay close attention to everything going on around you. What is the water doing? Weather changes? Time of year? What type of lake are you fishing? Fish strikes on the water, and even animal movement and sounds on the shore, become important. If you hear a hoot owl, the fish are getting ready to bite.

In life we should also pay close attention to all goings-on, especially the people we meet. Today's verse is one that pops into my mind every time someone I don't know asks for money or help. Could this be an angel? I always give or help. This is a special verse because it asks us to be cordial, gracious, friendly, and hospitable to folks we don't even know. I believe in angels. Whether you do or not, what a positive way to live your life.

> **TIP**
> When the dogwoods begin to bloom, that starts the spawn—males making beds, big girls eating spinnerbaits.

### JOHN 17:20

*"I do not pray for these alone, but also for those who
will believe in Me through their word."*

F ishing begins to get good around the middle of March
pretty much all over the South. The fish are in some
state of the spawn. A close friend and a capable foe this
time of the year is wind. We need it to warm the north
shorelines and put baitfish and
spawning bass where we want
them: on the end of our lines!

Because that wind can make lakes
very dangerous, it also creates prayers—
lots of prayers. In the entire chapter
surrounding today's verse, Jesus was
praying one long prayer for His disciples
and closest followers. And in this verse
He included you and me. He was asking
God to sanctify us, glorify us, protect us
from the devil, and give us eternal life
with Him in glory. I'm thankful for that
inclusion. How about you?

**TIP**

North banks
warm up
quicker due to
warm southerly
winds and
longer periods
of sunshine.

PSALM 91:14

*"Because he has set his love upon Me, therefore I will deliver him; I will set him on high, because he has known My name."*

One of my little rules of thumb is, if it's important to the bass, it's important to me. By the way, I have that same rule with Chris! If it's important to Chris . . . Whether it's food, cover, weather, or the spawn, figure out what is most important to that fish you're trying to catch, and your odds will increase dramatically.

How important is God to us? This psalm is talking about one who has a deep love for God and clings to Him. One who has personal knowledge of God's love and mercy. Someone who really trusts God. And here's the blessing for that person: honor directly from God, plus deliverance from trouble. I want to be that person. Do you?

## TIP

Be willing to change baits, colors, and techniques in early spring, as water and weather conditions change rapidly.

ROMANS 8:1

*There is therefore now no condemnation*
*to those who are in Christ Jesus.*

You don't have to be a pro to be able to make perfect casts. All you need to do is practice. Plus, when you're fishing, not all casts need to be perfect. But the more you practice, the better you will become. A good way to practice? Set up a rod or two in your house and practice a bit every day, pitching, casting, and flipping. You'll be amazed next time you go fishing! Difficult casts become easy!

It's even easier with God. Once we become united with Jesus by believing in Him, God does not condemn us for our sin. No sin, no matter how big or small, will be held against us. Jesus has paid for those sins in the past, right now, and in the future. A perfect cast takes practice. Believing in Jesus makes us perfect before almighty God, with no practice at all. I'll take that deal from here to eternity.

**TIP**
Bass hanging on the bottom are the easiest to catch.

EPHESIANS 6:11

*Put on the whole armor of God, that you may be*
*able to stand against the wiles of the devil.*

The equipment we put on a modern bass boat is mind-boggling. Three, four, five locators, trolling motor, jack plate, HydroWave, vents, bilge pump, aerators, light kits, cameras, and the young guys are saying, "Don't forget a stereo system!" Can I stop?

As Christians, we must be just as well equipped to stand against the devil. Our armor includes truth, righteousness, peace, faith, salvation, and finally, the sword of God's Holy Spirit. We should put this armor on every day and make every day a winner. The trick is to activate this battle armor with prayer. Personally, I believe prayer with praise is most effective. Are you ready?

**TIP**

One easy bait to help you read the bottom is a Tokyo Rig, which lets the weight make good contact with the bottom. It's perfect when the bottom is muddy or silty.

PROVERBS 22:1

*A good name is to be chosen rather than great riches.*

My buddy Wally Marshall, Mr. Crappie, is the best I know at naming fishing lures. Crappie Thunder, Slab Daddy, Slabalicious, and others. I named the Turbo Tail, which was a huge seller and tremendous fish catcher. Of course, names don't catch fish; the fish don't have any money. Catchy names catch fishermen.

The writer of Proverbs said a good name is about the most important thing you can own. He emphasized it is better than great riches. How do we get a good name? We can start with God's Ten Commandments: no lying, cheating, coveting, adultery, stealing, killing, and so on. We might want to cut out hatred, jealousy, envy, drunkenness, and so forth. Can we do all this? Yes, we can—once God puts His Holy Spirit inside us. That happens the moment we ask God to save us. Today, let's make the names we own even better.

**TIP**

Slow rolling a half-ounce Jimmy Houston Legends Spinnerbait in eight to twelve feet of water is dynamite right now.

NEHEMIAH 2:20

*The God of heaven Himself will prosper us.*

To prosper in tournament fishing is to catch a good limit and cash a check. To prosper at a career in fishing simply means making enough to pay the bills. To prosper in fishing is much more than money. It is memories and relationships that last long after the dollars are spent. It's teaching kids and spouses to fish. It's super times with lifelong friends.

God wants to prosper you in everything you do—family, church, job, health, and yes, even financially. Nehemiah was rebuilding the wall at Jerusalem. He was doing God's work when he confidently said, "God Himself will prosper us." Let us go about doing God's work today expecting God to prosper us, and, as He did for Nehemiah, God will! When we expect God to do something great, He usually does.

**TIP**
Become comfortable with and learn which lures work best under different water temperatures.

LUKE 4:40

*He laid His hands on every one of them and healed them.*

We hold a kid's fishing day every year at a lake on the grounds of the Expressway Auto Mall of America in Mount Vernon, Indiana. The kids catch mostly bluegill and catfish, plus an occasional bass or turtle. Of a few hundred kids, only a few win their age class and the trophies that go with it. But all receive a trophy just for being there. They didn't win them and may not even deserve them. But they are super excited to get those trophies.

In today's verse, Jesus was at Capernaum in Galilee at Peter's house. That evening, people started showing up with sick folks. Jesus healed them all. He didn't ask who had faith, who believed, or who could pay for the healing. He showed them God's love, mercy, and grace. And God's healing power is still available right now. Plus, just like at Peter's house, that healing is a free gift from God.

**TIP**
South Louisiana offers excellent winter fishing for reds, largemouth, trout, and flounder.

JOHN 11:35

*Jesus wept.*

There may be no crying in baseball, but I've sure seen plenty in fishing. Mostly tears of joy. Like when my friend Brian Latimer won his first FLW Tournament. But I have seen guys and gals cry when they learned they had just barely lost as well.

Today's verse is well-known as the Bible's shortest verse. But Jesus wept just before He performed one of His greatest miracles—raising his dead friend, Lazarus, back to life. Jesus walked on earth, all man and yet all God, performing incredible miracles. Even in death, we have full victory in Jesus. The grave can't hold us! The world can't defeat us. We may cry, we will have troubles, but in the end, just like Lazarus, we're going to walk right out of the grave. And as in baseball, there will be no crying in heaven. But there will be joy much greater than we have ever known.

**TIP**

When bass follow a jerkbait and don't bite, try different speeds and longer stops or pauses.

# MARCH 23

ROMANS 7:19

*The good that I will to do, I do not do; but the*
*evil I will not to do, that I practice.*

Sometimes fishing information from other fishermen can really help, but at times it can just add confusion.

I may know from my experience and knowledge that a spinnerbait or jig should be the best bait in a particular fishing situation. But someone else tells me he or she is catching fish on a crankbait. That clouds my mind, and the internal conflict often has me fishing the wrong way.

In today's verse, Paul had conflict too: he was fighting the battle of his flesh—controlled by sin and the devil—and his heart, soul, and mind—controlled by the laws of God. If Paul had this problem, you can bet you and I will also. Like Paul, we are carnal, we are weak in the flesh, and, yes, we will fail. But Jesus has paid for those sins as well. His grace is greater than all our sins.

**TIP**
The fish will spawn heavily on a new moon at water temps above 60 degrees Fahrenheit.

JIMMY HOUSTON

DEUTERONOMY 20:3

*Do not let your heart faint, do not be afraid,*
*and do not tremble or be terrified.*

O ne of the surest ways to fail in fishing is to be afraid to
fail. Tournament fishermen fall into this trap often.
I've done so myself. The best fishermen
will be the ones who gamble—the
ones who leave "honey holes" that are
not producing. They try areas they haven't
seen in years, lures they didn't throw in practice, and basically trust their own confidence
and ability.

> **TIP**
> Search out
> shallow flats
> that touch
> deeper water.
> A bend in a
> creek or river
> is perfect.

God was saying in today's verse to never
be afraid or tremble as long as your trust and
faith are in God. There is nothing left to fear.
God will always go with you to fight against
whatever the enemy may be. Most Christians
need more faith. I need more, and I'm thinking you need more. We get that through past experience
with God and through hearing the message about Christ.

PROVERBS 13:11

*Wealth gained by dishonesty will be diminished,*
*but he who gathers by labor will increase.*

Successful fishing is about a lot of things, but one common denominator for all great fishermen is effort—hard work. Are the best fishermen lucky? No more than anyone else. But the harder I work, the luckier I get.

Wealth and riches are talked about often in the Bible. Wealth is gained in various ways. I've seen Christians chastised simply because they were successful or wealthy. God created wealth for many of His chosen—Abraham, Noah, Joseph, David, Solomon, Jacob, Hezekiah, and this list could go on and on.

God is still doing so today, but He sums up what He will bless, what He will increase: wealth gained by labor; wealth gained honestly. God is a rewarder of hard work, and He loves honesty. Let's get to work! Let's do it honestly, and let's praise God for the rewards.

**TIP**

Use bigger baits this time of the year—bigger baits equal bigger bass.

LUKE 8:50

*"Do not be afraid; only believe, and she will be made well."*

Sometimes we come upon a spot that looks so good we know there's fish there. It may be a point, a structure near deep water, or a particularly great-looking dock. I have found spots like this in tournament practice and didn't catch any fish there, only to recheck those spots in competition and whack 'em there. I really believed in that spot!

Many of the miracles Jesus did required no belief, no faith on the part of the person asking for help. The one in today's scripture, where Jesus brought a young girl back to life, did require belief. Or did it? A couple of verses down it says, "They ridiculed Him" because she was dead (v. 53)—"they" being the girl's parents and Peter, James, and John. *Wow.* He brought the little girl back to life anyway—but only after He had put them and their unbelief out of the room. Our miracle might just be waiting for us to put unbelief out of the room.

**TIP**

On older jigs, use small wire or a paper clip to hold the old skirts together.

# MARCH 27

2 KINGS 18:7

*The LORD was with him; he prospered wherever he went.*

Usually, right before massive storms, fishing is fantastic. It does seem the bigger the hurricane, the more severe and widespread the thunderstorms are, the better the fish bite. The weather generally comes in with very low barometric pressure that rises rapidly as the storms get closer. In these cases the strike zones of the bass grow very large, and you are able to catch fish everywhere.

Would you like to be successful everywhere? You don't have to rely on the weather. Today's verse is talking about King Hezekiah, but it could just as easily be talking about you and me. Hezekiah prospered because he relied totally on God. Our hope needs to be exclusively on God in every situation. We obey Him. We praise Him. We honor Him in all we do. When we do all this, we make it easy for God to prosper us.

**TIP**

Figure out where most fish are in the spawn to whack 'em today. Remember, it changes daily.

REVELATION 13:16

*He causes all, both small and great, rich and poor, free and slave,*
*to receive a mark on their right hand or on their foreheads.*

As we move into the spawning season, we all get excited about being able to catch a few big fat female bass. We start looking for those light spots on the bottom where a bass has made a bed. We mark these spots on our GPS to fish later, often using different color marks depending on size. (A great pair of Jimmy Houston sunglasses is a must for seeing spawning bass.)

When John wrote today's verse from Revelation, slaves, soldiers, and even religious cults were commonly marked with tattoos as identification marks. Today we see the possibility of marking someone with computer chips implanted within one's hand or head. Marking a spawning bass on a GPS is good. We may catch that bass. The mark of Satan on our bodies or in our bodies means we belong to the devil, and that's very bad. Let's stand strong in Jesus.

**TIP**

Big spawning bass that you can't see are less pressured and easier to catch.

## MARCH 29

JOSHUA 14:11

*As yet I am as strong this day as on the day that Moses sent*
*me; just as my strength was then, so now is my strength.*

As I write this book, I am seventy-six years old, so today's verse means a lot to me. I am still strong, and may go back and fish more tournaments. My buddy Larry Walker, who is about my age, says he can do everything as well now as he could at thirty-five. I really believe I can too.

Caleb, in this scripture, was talking to his longtime buddy Joshua who had become the leader of the children of Israel. These two men had spied out the promised land years earlier and had encouraged the Israelites to take ownership of it. Caleb was eighty-five on the day he spoke the words in today's verse. If you've got a few years on you, you need a hero. May I suggest Caleb and Joshua, spies who gave a good report and were given health into old age by God?

> **TIP**
> Keep fishing long into your life! Walk to keep your legs in shape.

JAMES 1:14

*Each one is tempted when he is drawn away*
*by his own desires and enticed.*

Little tiny jigs with small soft plastic attached have always been nearly irresistible to fish. I remember finishing second place to Jerry Rhyne in a B.A.S.S. tournament on Lake Ouachita in Arkansas back in 1981. My fish came on what today is called a Ned rig, a tiny jig and hook with a small worm attached. Want to entice a finicky bass? Try this combination.

In Greek the phrase *drawn away* describes animals trapped and drawn away to their deaths. *Enticed* is a fishing term meaning "caught with bait." Like a fish with the little Ned rig, we are often tempted by something that seems small at first. Then we feed the temptation with our own desires, such as lust, the sin of the flesh leading to adultery, and lust for other worldly pleasures and things. As with the animals and fish, something small often leads to death, so turn to God when you face temptation.

**TIP**

It's always good to wet your knots on monofilament line before clenching them down.

# MARCH 31

LUKE 4:30

*Passing through the midst of them, He went His way.*

If you ask fishermen about their biggest fish, most can tell you in a heartbeat. They will also quickly tell you of the big one that got away. The devil often thought he had Jesus (the Big One) caught, ready to kill. But Jesus came to earth on His Father's timetable, and with His protection.

Today's scripture tells the end of the story when a crowd attempted to throw Jesus over a cliff and kill Him. He simply walked through the crowd (kind of like parting the water) and went His way. This is the first of several miraculous escapes by Jesus. Jesus knew His mission from His Father was to die for our sins. But He also knew that the time was of His Father's choosing. You and I know we will die. Can I tell you that time is of God's choosing as well? No virus or illness will change that. Only God can!

**TIP**
Put a foam ear plug inside soft plastic tubes to hold scent.

APRIL

## PROVERBS 12:26

*The righteous should choose his friends carefully.*

Choosing the right bait is obviously one of the most important decisions we all make. If you only had five lures, you would have a 20 percent chance of picking the best one every time. What if you have five hundred lures? Now it's a tougher decision. Thankfully, you don't need to pick the very best one. But you also don't want to pick number 384!

Pick a bait with some red and/or blue in it that imitates the dominant baitfish in the area.

Choosing lures is tough, but choosing friends is even harder—and a lot more important. The advice in today's scripture becomes easier as we get older; it is more difficult for younger people to discern who is a worthy friend. The rest of today's proverb adds that the ways of the wicked will lead us astray. So choose friends that will build you up and who are positive and honest—friends that will celebrate your success and your walk with God.

**TIP**

Search out shell beds in natural Florida lakes for schools of bass.

JOHN 3:35

*The Father loves the Son, and has given all things into His hand.*

The easiest way to get your kids and grandkids into fishing is, quite simply, take them fishing. I don't even think they actually need to be big enough to fish, just big enough to go. What we are giving our kids when we take them fishing is worth more than gold. We are giving them a completely different set of moral and ethical values than they learn anywhere else. We are giving them patience, understanding, love, and *time*. We are giving them *us*! Because we love them, we are giving them everything we can. How important is that?

In today's verse, John the Baptist said God had given everything to His Son, Jesus. And Jesus in turn can give all to us. The most important thing is eternal life, given to those of us who believe in Him.

**TIP**
Use a wooden toothpick and stick it through a swimbait just above the hook bend to keep your swimbait from tearing on the hookset.

ACTS 26:13

*I saw a light from heaven, brighter than the sun, shining around me.*

Meeting Ray Scott, founder of B.A.S.S., and Forrest Wood, founder of Ranger Boats, during the 1968 B.A.S.S. tournament on Lake Eufaula, Alabama, changed my life. These two would become giants in the bass-fishing industry. Becoming friends with these two gentlemen strengthened that change.

Today's verse is about the conversion of Saul, who became Paul and wrote much of the New Testament. He had a life-changing personal encounter with Jesus Himself on his way to Damascus to arrest Christians and put them in chains. And on top of that, Jesus preached a minisermon to him and anointed Paul as a preacher to the Gentiles. On his knees and blinded, Paul surrendered his life to Jesus. This personal encounter is what we, too, must experience. We might not hear Jesus speak out loud. But the moment we surrender, God puts His Spirit inside us, and He speaks to us daily.

**TIP**

Early season crappie fishing is awesome in most Florida lakes.

ROMANS 12:17
*Repay no one evil for evil.*

Tournament fishermen are a pretty close-knit bunch. Sure, there are some grudges and an occasional disagreement about fishing water. But we support one another, and when someone actually does something questionable that has to be addressed, we pretty much keep it within our small group. Even on social media platforms the pros are mostly a class act.

In today's verse, Paul was speaking to mostly Gentile Roman Christians and showing them how to live a righteous life by blessing those who cursed them, living in peace with others, feeding the hungry, loving one another, not avenging, and overcoming evil with good. If only all of us could live this way. Can I tell you something? We can! We can be righteous because God is righteous, and His Spirit is inside every Christian. Lean on His righteousness today, and let's make this world a better place one Christian at a time.

**TIP**
Pair an Aqua-Vu underwater camera with your Garmin fish finder to learn more about what you are seeing on your locator.

# APRIL 5

JOB 19:25

*I know that my Redeemer lives, and He
shall stand at last on the earth.*

Tournament fishermen depend on sponsors. Without sponsorship, most if not all tournament anglers cannot compete. I know I couldn't. We have had some situations where very well-known pros have quit the game after losing a couple of major sponsors. They simply couldn't pay the bills to keep competing.

Have you ever been in a tough financial situation like that? Job was, and worse. He lost everything but his wife and his life. All his children, all wealth, all associates, all health, all possessions, all gone. Total desperation! How would you react? Would you blame someone? Blame God? We can see in today's verse that at Job's most dreadful moment, his faith seemed the greatest. God was his Redeemer, and he stood on that belief. We will have trials. We will have pain. But we know that our Redeemer lives!

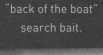

**TIP**
A Tokyo Rig is an exceptional "back of the boat" search bait.

PSALM 37:4

*Delight yourself also in the LORD, and He shall*
*give you the desires of your heart.*

Fishermen look at Bass Pro Shops like a big candy store. I've got to admit, it's true for me as well. My buddy Johnny Morris, founder of Bass Pro, is just as bad as you and me. Johnny has already bought all that neat hunting and fishing stuff in there. He already owns it.

You know the thing I really like about today's scripture? It says God will give you the desires of your heart. We don't have to earn them or work for them. All we need to do is delight in the Lord, honor Him, study His Word, praise Him, put Him first. This is easy. This is great! How do we know when a blessing is from God? It comes unexpectedly and seems to drop out of heaven. When God's time is right, He gives us the desires of our hearts.

**TIP**
I like to fish with a 7'3" medium-heavy Jimmy Houston Blaze Series rod when fishing with a Whopper Plopper.

PSALM 118:28
*You are my God, and I will praise You; You*
*are my God, I will exalt You.*

Everybody has their favorite fish. I guess the most popular in America is crappie. Many love bass, and there are lots of catfishermen out there. Trout, stripers, white bass, wipers, walleye, muskie, gar; every species has its die-hard followers. Me, I love 'em all!

But when we love something too much—like power, wealth, or popularity—it can become like worshiping another god. We must be careful to give our praise to the only God, the God who hung the moon and stars, and individually call Him "my God." More importantly, He calls us His children. And He loves us with a love that never fades or ends. God is working in our lives every day and for our good. But we praise God for who He is and not for what He does for us. We exalt God because He is worthy of exaltation and worship.

**TIP**
Search out isolated targets to fish—stumps, rocks, docks, duck blinds, laydowns, and so on.

PHILIPPIANS 4:4

*Rejoice in the Lord always. Again I will say, rejoice!*

I fished a tournament once with NASCAR legend and great friend Bobby Allison. Bobby and I had previously done a television show on Lake Guntersville in Alabama. The magic of this tournament (NASCAR drivers paired with pro fishermen) was where the tournament was held: Disney World. It's one of the most joy-filled places in the world. Bobby and I won the tournament, the trophies, and $10,000 apiece. We were more than happy!

Today's verse is one of my favorites. Notice it doesn't say be sad in the Lord or be worried, afraid, or hateful. It says *rejoice.* Be really, really happy. When should we rejoice? Always. Our rejoicing is not related to our circumstances. We rejoice because of our unchanging relationship with Jesus. We rejoice today, tomorrow, and forever.

> **TIP**
> Don't overlook stumps in deeper water in rivers with silty bottoms for bass spawning beds.

REVELATION 3:19

*"As many as I love, I rebuke and chasten.*
*Therefore be zealous and repent."*

One of my cardinal rules in getting spouses and kids into fishing is, don't gripe at them! Now, that's a rule most would agree with. But there are certain things you must lovingly drill into their minds, like wearing a life jacket and paying close attention to others when casting so as not to hook something other than a fish. How we teach, how we correct, becomes almost as important as the lesson. Give your total time and attention to them. Don't criticize; teach. Don't complain; exhort. The joy of seeing them catch fish is worth it all.

In today's verse Jesus was speaking to the church at Laodicea, one He called lukewarm, like tepid and bad-tasting water. Basically, Jesus was saying there were no true believers in that church. It's not much different today in many churches. Jesus is exhorting you and me to get fired up and repent.

**TIP**

An Alberto knot is good for tying a leader to braid.

2 TIMOTHY 1:12

*I know whom I have believed and am persuaded that He is able to keep what I have committed to Him until that Day.*

There are certain beliefs in bass fishing that we trust, day in and day out. I call these rules of thumb. Like, "Fish a spinnerbait or buzzbait if it's raining"; "Throw a crankbait when the water level is falling"; "Fish the heaviest cover you can find close to deep water"; "Wide wobble cranks work well in high-pressure lakes." Obviously, every fisherman has a bunch of these. They are truths we have come to believe.

Today's verse perfectly sums up what we as Christians need to believe. Our relationship with God begins when we make Him our Lord and will continue through eternity. We have totally given our lives to God now and forever. We can be bold in Christ and live in confidence of His protection—and we will receive our reward in heaven with God Himself.

**TIP**

To add scale patterns to crankbaits, use drywall tape and spray paint.

PSALM 37:11

*The meek shall inherit the earth, and shall delight*
*themselves in the abundance of peace.*

Finesse fishing has always been productive. It can put fish in the boat when other techniques won't. The key is light line and small lures. It also helps to slow down a bit and really relax when you're fishing this way. For me, that's pretty hard. I love power fishing, and it's a little tough to slow down and take it nice and easy. When I do, it generally pays off well: I catch the fish and find some peace in the process.

Today's verse talks about finding peace through being meek. Here, God was not saying being meek means being a pushover. God was talking about being good, and not only avoiding evil but not envying those who seem to prosper while being evil, lying, cheating, stealing, and living ungodly lives. Their success and riches will go away. In addition, so many of them will have tremendous strife in their lives! The good, the righteous, will have peace.

**TIP**
Search out small state and city lakes for giant bass.

NEHEMIAH 8:10

*Do not sorrow, for the joy of the LORD is your strength.*

Tournament fishing teaches us that not every day is going to be a good one. The winds and water will not always be the way we want them to be. We often need to reach down and muster up that something extra when we wake up to a strong, freezing north wind with rain. That's when tournament fishing becomes a real challenge. The most challenging competition days are the ones right after a really bad weather day, when there is no hope to win any money. Bad conditions multiply the bad performance.

Life is often just like that, bad stacking up on bad. I've found the only way we can get through these days is to realize what we have in Jesus—how much God has done and will continue to do for us. Today's verse says the joy of the Lord is our strength, and this allows us to go face the day with the right attitude.

**TIP**

A constant, steady retrieve at medium speed will work most days with a ChatterBait.

REVELATION 20:14 KJV

*And death and hell were cast into the lake of fire.*

Bass, catfish, crappie, bluegill, and many other fish are very protective of their spawning areas. They will fight off just about anything to protect their eggs and then later their young. We, of course, can use this to our advantage during this magic time of the year to catch these fish. It's also the time of year when most fish I catch cheat death because this is the time to practice conservation—catch-and-release, barbless hooks, and keeping only a few small male fish.

None of us will cheat death here on earth; we all experience it, and one of the saddest things we can do is attend a funeral of a friend who we think may not be saved. When God isn't mentioned in a funeral, it's very disheartening. If you have a friend or family member who may not know Jesus, tell that loved one. As today's scripture shows, Jesus has defeated the ultimate enemy—death!

**TIP**
Place a small piece of foam inside a tube for extra flotation. It can also hold scent.

2 CORINTHIANS 4:18

*For the things which are seen are temporary, but the things which are not seen are eternal.*

Some of the best spots to catch fish are places where we have caught them before! Some of the worst spots to fish are the places where we have caught them before. Whaaat? Actually, pretty simple—most spots will produce fish only under certain temporary conditions. The right weather, a certain water level or water temperature, a single time of the year. A few places will hold fish no matter what. These are those honey holes we treasure!

This verse about temporary things, I believe, is telling us that how we see or think here on earth is not the same way God is looking at things. We see ourselves broke; God says we have all we need. We see ourselves unattractive; God says we're beautiful! We see ourselves weak and powerless; God says we are mighty heroes. Today, let's not be too concerned about what we see but focus on what God says we are.

**TIP**

In colder water, drag a jig more than hopping it.

COLOSSIANS 3:2

*Set your mind on things above, not on things on the earth.*

I define a *structure* as any object that is different from or breaks up the water's bottom or surface. This can be rocks, brush, docks, humps, road-beds, creek channels, even an old sunken boat or bridge. Obviously, some structures can be better than others.

Our thoughts are like those structures: some are better than others. Today's scripture reminds us that we can set our minds on what is really important in our lives. By focusing our thoughts on things above, we get rid of evil desires, covetousness, and filth. We are less prone to anger, wrath, malice, and bad language. The list is long.

So what do we set our minds on? What should be our inner disposition? Kindness, humility, meekness, tender mercy, forgiveness, patience, and love, which is most important. Thinking on and practicing these heavenly traits will make us better husbands, wives, fathers, mothers, friends, and people.

**TIP**
Ripraps are some of the best and easiest structures to locate.

ROMANS 8:35

*Who shall separate us from the love of Christ? Shall tribulation, or distress, or persecution, or famine, or nakedness, or peril, or sword?*

I had always been a Bass Pro guy and bought all my fishing and hunting stuff there. When my buddy and Bass Pro founder Johnny Morris acquired Cabela's, it was difficult for me, and I'm sure many others, to think of the two popular sporting goods stores together. I had only been in a couple of Cabela's ever, but I had shopped in basically every Bass Pro in the nation! However, Johnny successfully joined together the two companies.

When we became believers, we were joined together with Christ by His love. In today's scripture, Paul was telling us that Jesus loves us through our most difficult and trying situations. Nothing we can experience will stop that love. Nothing ever created—no government or power. Even death will not separate us from Jesus' love for us.

**TIP**

Multiple casts— as many as nine or ten—at the same piece of structure will produce on pressured lakes.

2 THESSALONIANS 3:13

*As for you, brethren, do not grow weary in doing good.*

To become a really good fisherman, you'll need to get good with all the tools of fishing: casting and spinning reels, electronics, trolling motors, lures, knots. It's quite a bit to learn and become skilled with. It's easy with the equipment you love to use (a certain lure, technique, or reel), but much more difficult learning something you don't like. To be successful, you can't grow weary. You can't give up.

**TIP**

Keep your lure in a potential strike-zone area as long as possible. Be patient in those fish-catching spots.

In today's verse, Paul was telling the church at Thessalonica to continue with their ministry of giving even though some people on the receiving end had quit working and simply lived by taking handouts and charity. Although that may still be the case today, many people are in true need and benefit greatly from our generosity. So don't stop giving or doing good. Never get tired of helping.

JEREMIAH 32:27

*"Behold, I am the LORD, the God of all flesh.*
*Is there anything too hard for Me?"*

Cold fronts really affect fishing, especially bass fishing. The day before the front is usually a dynamite day to be on the water. The day of the front, the fishing conditions may be awful. And then, the day after the front, calm water, bluebird skies, and some of the hardest fishing ever. Generally, accurate casting into heavy cover will produce. It's some really difficult fishing.

In today's verse, storms and hard times were coming for God's people. God had instructed Jeremiah to buy a piece of land and to seal the deed and title. Jeremiah obeyed but questioned God because he knew Babylon would soon conquer and destroy Jerusalem. God was assuring Jeremiah He would bring His people back to possess this land. When we honor God through the storms, He will even bless our kids and grandkids!

**TIP**
Bare clay points will almost always hold smallmouth bass, particularly in the spring.

PROVERBS 27:20

*Hell and Destruction are never full; so the*
*eyes of man are never satisfied.*

One of my longtime friends and guide on Sam Rayburn
Reservoir in Texas was Marvin Baker. Marvin was
also an exceptionally good tournament fisherman and
won several times. One such victory was a
B.A.S.S. event on Sam Rayburn.
I finished second and Roland
Martin was third. After the final
weigh-in, Marvin was telling Roland and
me about losing this giant bass—"Man, if
I would have just caught that fish." I just
laughed and said, "Marvin, you can't do any
better than first!"

Man's dreams and desires are insatiable.
We seem to always want more, and—you
bet—I'm just as guilty as everyone else. But
here's where we need to be careful. God gives
us success. He gives us victory. God gives us
everything we have, including our very next
breath. We need to thank God for that every day.

**TIP**

When pitching
to standing
timber in
deeper water,
stop the drop of
your bait about
every five feet.

PSALM 139:14

*I will praise You, for I am fearfully and wonderfully made.*

When we graduated from college, Chris and I opened an insurance agency. With God's help and eighty to a hundred hours of hard work from each of us every week, we built the agency from nothing into a successful business we later sold. That enabled us to become more involved in what became a fishing career. We still worked eighty to a hundred hours a week. And now, more than fifty years later, we still work these long weeks.

How and why do we do that? Because that's the way God made us. He didn't make us to fail. He made us to thrive! And just as important, He gave us the health to be able to do it. God didn't make everyone this way, just as he didn't make us all six foot five or give us all a voice like Elvis. But I believe He made us all to be the very best we could be. Praise God! Let's all do our best.

**TIP**

Fish move as conditions and seasons change. Try to figure out where the fish are going.

JOB 41:11

*"Who has preceded Me, that I should pay him?*
*Everything under heaven is Mine."*

Preceding bass spawning, the fish go through several states before they actually make it to a bed. Understanding these key pre-spawn and pre-pre-spawn activities is vital. When we know that they stage on points in eight to ten feet of water, that they travel along north shorelines, that they like gentle-sloping banks, we have just a few of the many keys that help us catch 'em! That's the reward for our knowledge.

In life our reward comes from God. In today's verse, God was telling Job just how big a God He really is. He has no reason or need to pay for anything. He created it all, and He owns it all. He has no earthly reason to pay (or reward) us for anything we say or do. But He does. He does because of His great love, His mercy, His grace. He did reward Job, and He will reward you and me.

**TIP**
Use floating jerkbaits to blind cast around bedding areas.

JAMES 4:7

*Submit to God. Resist the devil and he will flee from you.*

The highly pressured lakes we have today require a different approach to be successful, especially during the spring, when fishing pressure is the greatest because lots of folks are fishing. We need to become a little more of a hunter on these crowded waters. We need to become stealthier and wear darker clothing, and it is important to run our trolling motors on a slower speed. Literally slip up on the fish to keep from running them off.

We don't want to run the fish off, but we definitely need to chase the devil away! As you can see from today's verse, we do this by submitting to God: lining up under His authority, doing His will, obeying Him, and honoring Him. The really scary thing is, we either serve God or we serve Satan. I can't see much in between. Humble yourself today before the God who hung the moon, and watch the devil run.

**TIP**
Concentrate on the shady sides of boat docks with spinnerbaits and topwaters that you can cast accurately.

PROVERBS 28:1
*The wicked flee when no one pursues, but*
*the righteous are bold as a lion.*

Tournament bass fishing is an extremely honest game to play. Over the years, we have had a few bend the rules, but most were caught pretty quickly and penalized severely. Most intentional cheaters are banned for life. When someone is penalized for a rule violation, it is usually an accidental breaking of a rule. And get this— the angler generally turns himself or herself in and takes the penalty, even when it sometimes costs an entire day's catch!

Today's proverb seems to be speaking about wicked or evil people who have guilty consciences and are always looking over their shoulders, as if someone is chasing them. The righteous, on the other hand, have clear consciences, with all sins wiped clean by the blood of Jesus. If you have sins on your mind today, confess them to God. They are cleared when you make Jesus your Lord and Savior.

**TIP**
Since they sit so low to the water, be on the lookout for kayaks late in the evening.

PSALM 103:5

*. . . so that your youth is renewed like the eagle's.*

Eagles are expert fishers. We have seen pictures and watched videos of these beautiful birds swooping down to pick their catch up out of the water. They are fast and strong. It's amazing how big a fish they can carry.

Today's verse compares a righteous person blessed by God to that magnificent eagle. Eagles live long lives. Like eagles, the young possess speed and strength. I don't know about you, but I'll take a renewing of youth from God every day! This psalm is saying we can and will stay young longer under God's blessings. Does this really work? I believe it 100 percent. Just take a look at a few of my fishing buddies who have some years on them—Bill Dance, Roland Martin, and Hank Parker. God sure has renewed their youth, and they soar like eagles!

**TIP**
Really huge bass spend most of their time suspended over open water but still usually related to structure—near a tree, over a brush pile, or close to a channel.

## COLOSSIANS 3:23

*Whatever you do, do it heartily, as to the Lord and not to men.*

Our kids, Jamie and Sherri, grew up being on television. With nearly fifty years on national television, we've now fished with grandkids and great-grandkids as well.

One of the common problems with kids in front of cameras, or just in front of people in general, is them being really quiet and subdued, barely speaking or speaking really low and with no emotion. I've told them all, "Hey, do this with *enthusiasm*! Speak up! Get excited! Smile! Be happy!"

There is nothing that we should get more excited about than our relationship with God. God was telling us in today's verse to get excited. Get enthusiastic at whatever you do, as if you were doing it for God. So, whatever you're doing today, do it heartily, with *enthusiasm*. You are doing it for God Himself.

**TIP**

Use an Aqua-Vu underwater camera to really learn what is there in deeper, clearer lakes.

1 CORINTHIANS 13:13

*Now abide faith, hope, love, these three;*
*but the greatest of these is love.*

The more exact we become in fishing, the more fish we will catch. What is this exactness all about? It's about accurate casts, fishing structures properly, and casting angles. It's about reading electronics, operating your trolling motor, and even having your mind in the right place. Exactness is relatively easy in shallow water but much more diffi-cult in deeper water.

Today's verse names three tenets of Christianity that are easy and pretty enjoya-ble when things are going well: faith, hope, and love. But as we move into deeper water and things get tough, we need help on all three fronts. Faith and hope last only while we walk this earth. They are totally ful-filled in heaven. Love, that's forever. God's love is perfect. Ours will be perfected. I'm asking God to increase me in all three. How about you?

## TIP

An underspin (a jig paired with a smaller spinner blade underneath) with a shad-colored Luck-E-Swim trailer works well after the spawn.

# APRIL 27

## 1 CORINTHIANS 13:8

*Love never fails. But whether there are prophecies, they
will fail; whether there are tongues, they will cease;
whether there is knowledge, it will vanish away.*

Years ago I named a cove on Lake Tenkiller in
Oklahoma "Never Fail" because it didn't matter when
we fished it—we caught fish. Whatever the time of the
year or the type of weather, be it morning, evening, or
middle of the day, we always caught a fish in that cove.
We still call it by that same name, Never Fail, after more
than fifty years!

Paul was saying in today's scripture that prophecies, tongues, and
knowledge will either fail, cease, disappear,
or be abolished eventually. But the one item
that will never fail is love! With that in mind,
we need to make love the centerpiece of our
lives, our families, our jobs, our church, our
nation, our relationship with God. When we
do that, how can we fail?

## TIP
Small jig
and worm
combinations
(Ned rigs) work
best on dirty
bottoms.

MARK 4:40

*[Jesus] said to them, "Why are you so fearful?*
*How is it that you have no faith?"*

The Great Lakes provide some of the best fishing in this wonderful country of ours. Bass, walleye, salmon, catfish, muskie, and the list goes on. But they are almost oceans and not lakes. Big, wide expanses of water that get rough and dangerous in a hurry. The Sea of Galilee (also known as Lake Gennesaret) is a freshwater lake much like our Great Lakes, except it doesn't have very good fishing.

Jesus spoke the words in today's verse after being awakened from a deep sleep by the disciples as their boat crossed this huge lake. This storm was so fierce that the boat was sinking. Jesus had been preaching and healing all day and was exhausted. He simply spoke to the storm and it stopped. The Creator who hung and created the moon and stars was in their boat! Is Jesus in your boat? Storms will come. Ask Jesus to come aboard your life today.

**TIP**

Begin fishing topwater baits when the water temperature hits 60 degrees Fahrenheit.

ROMANS 8:11

*He who raised Christ from the dead will also give life to your mortal bodies through His Spirit who dwells in you.*

Swimbaits have become popular with all fishermen in both freshwater and saltwater. They look so real, and there are so many ways to fish them. Although not legal in the bigger tournaments, the umbrella or Alabama rig is still one of the most effective ways to catch really giant fish. This rig, with five or more swimbaits on jig heads, imitates a small, vulnerable school of shad. Bass can't resist attacking this bait.

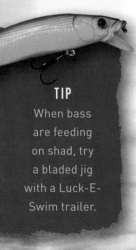

If we are not saved, our mortal bodies are vulnerable to attacks by Satan. We live for the flesh and its worldly sins and develop carnal minds. Once saved, though, we receive the Spirit of God. This gives our mortal bodies life, and we begin to become the kind of people God intended us to be. Are you saved?

**TIP**

When bass are feeding on shad, try a bladed jig with a Luck-E-Swim trailer.

PROVERBS 15:15

*He who is of a merry heart has a continual feast.*

As crappie finish spawning, they become much harder to catch than when they were lined up on the bank, back in tiny coves and pockets, busy making baby crappie. One of the keys to locating them is to find the shad. Crappie feast on spawning shad. If the lake you are fishing has grass, that's the first place the crappie will go to catch the shad that spawn there. It's like an all-you-can-eat feast for crappie.

Our hearts' desire is a feast of happiness, and today's scripture tells us how to have that. Our hearts must be joyous regardless of conditions. We must see the good in everything and everyone and live life with enthusiasm. It is important that we live exceptional lives and allow the fruit of God's Spirit to guide our thoughts and words. Make your heart merry today, and sit down to a banquet of happiness and joy!

**TIP**

When you find male bass on beds, catch the big females out front in five to eight feet of water on big spinnerbaits.

MAY

JOB 42:6

*Therefore I abhor myself, and repent in dust and ashes.*

My greatest disappointment in tournament fishing was the Super B.A.S.S. event on Chickamauga Lake, Chattanooga, Tennessee. I failed to win the tournament, when I should have easily won. On the final tournament day, we were not allowed to lock down the river as I had throughout the tournament. I was so down and so disappointed even after winning the biggest prize of the year—Angler of the Year. Chris corrected my thinking and my heart.

In today's scripture, Job had been corrected by God. He was still a broken and sick man, destitute, ashamed, and humiliated. But he realized God was still real and his only hope. When things are going wrong in your life, even if it's not your fault, repent of any sin you have. Watch God start making things better.

**TIP**

Natural structures such as rocks, brush, ditches, and channel swings are generally better than man-made cover. Random cover is best.

JOHN 5:17

*Jesus answered them, "My Father has been working until now, and I have been working."*

I hear folks talking about how much hard work it is to fish an Alabama or umbrella rig, how it wears them out, and how quickly they have to stop fishing that rig. The biggest problem is most use a really heavy rod; some even use flippin' sticks! It is best to use a 7' or 7'3" medium-heavy rod with fifty-pound test braided line.

God is not bothered by hard work. God never sleeps. In today's verse, Jesus was affirming that He and God are busy doing God's work. Rest assured; if you belong to Jesus, He is busy right now working on your behalf. He's setting up the right situations, the right timing, the right people to make your life better and to help you achieve your dreams. When you trust Jesus, He starts working for your good. When Jesus is working on our side, nothing can stop us.

**TIP**
Nose-hook soft plastics to get extra action in open water.

EPHESIANS 2:7

*. . . that in the ages to come He might show the exceeding riches of His grace in His kindness toward us in Christ Jesus.*

It is important to understand the strike zone of a bass under the varying circumstances we fish. The strike zone is the area around a fish we must get our bait into to get a strike. The larger the strike zone, the easier it is to catch the fish. Conversely, as a fish's strike zone gets smaller, we must slow down and make deadly accurate casts. Those days with large strike zones are pure heaven, with riches of fish!

**TIP**
Riprap corners are the best, but always fish the ends as well.

Today's verse is surely speaking of heaven as being God's exceeding riches. I'm wondering why God wants us in heaven anyway. I think it may be the same reason He saves us in the first place—for His glory. Heaven just might be the most important thing on every Christian's mind. Heaven is the exceeding riches of God's enormous and eternal love for us. It points to a love and grace that has no bounds.

COLOSSIANS 3:8

*Now you yourselves are to put off all these: anger, wrath,*
*malice, blasphemy, filthy language out of your mouth.*

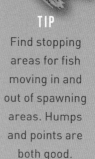

All man-made lakes create current flow. These lakes are made by damming up rivers and creeks. Obviously, what comes in the river must flow out the dam. This creates current, and usually the more current, the better the fishing. Concentrate on areas where this water flows: points, humps, ledges, and bends in the creek channels. All these are excellent.

Just like water flowing through the dam, what is in our hearts and minds will flow from our mouths. We all slip up at times (ever had a really bad backlash or lost a really big fish?), but God creates in each of us a new person when we are saved. This is like taking off dirty clothes and putting on new, clean ones. Just as a current makes fishing better, we become better when we are saved.

**TIP**
Find stopping areas for fish moving in and out of spawning areas. Humps and points are both good.

HEBREWS 10:25

*. . . not forsaking the assembling of ourselves together, as*
*is the manner of some, but exhorting one another.*

All tournament fishermen develop a game plan for each day. Obviously, it's a moving target throughout each day and very seldom works perfectly as planned, but it's always smart to have a plan going in. Plan your fishing trip around the type of water you are fishing, the time of the year, the water conditions, and the weather. Without a doubt, you will have a better fishing trip.

I have heard it said for years, "I can worship God just as well on the lake as I can in church." I do worship and praise God a lot on the water and in the woods. But did you catch the last three words in today's verse? Exhorting one another. That means encouraging and comforting one another—in person. The preaching, teaching, and praying become part of our game plan for tomorrow, next week, next year, eternity. See you in church!

**TIP**
Water temperature is even more important this time of year; find warmer water.

PSALM 128:1

*Blessed is everyone who fears the LORD, who walks in His ways.*

A trailer hook on a spinnerbait will definitely catch you a few more fish. Of all the tournaments I've won on a spinnerbait, I can't think of any I would have won without that trailer hook. Those few fish on the trailer hook were the difference between winning and not winning. But trailer hooks get hung up a lot, and many people are just afraid to fish them.

That's a negative kind of fear. Today's verse clearly explains what fear of the Lord is about—a positive kind of fear; it's about walking in God's ways. It's about doing God's will. It's about being blessed! The remaining verses in Psalm 128 tell us exactly how we will be blessed, with plenty to eat, with prosperity, with a spouse, children, and grandkids! I'm signed up for those supurb blessings. How about you? Let's walk in His ways.

**TIP**
When things go wrong while fishing, don't let the devil get in your head. Stay calm and have fun—you are fishing.

HEBREWS 3:8

*Do not harden your hearts as in the rebellion.*

It's critical when fishing to find a hard bottom. Obviously, in shallow water, we can simply stick our rod tips down and check it out. Our locators can also tell us whether we are fishing a soft or hard bottom. Just like other structures, small areas of a hard bottom often hold big numbers of fish. Keep your eyes on that fish locator. The hard bottom might be a roadbed, gravel, or a rock pile, but most likely it is holding bass.

Today's verse speaks of a hard heart that just won't let God in. The Holy Spirit is giving a history lesson about the Israelites' forty years in the desert, when many never allowed God and His Holy Spirit inside their hearts. Are we guilty of that today? You bet! When we show unbelief, when we disobey, when we don't go to church— anytime we don't allow God completely inside our hearts. Let's soften our hearts today; a soft heart is where we'll find the biggest spiritual catch.

**TIP**
Tubes are easy to skip under boat docks.

DANIEL 10:12

*Do not fear, Daniel, for from the first day that you set your heart to understand, and to humble yourself before your God, your words were heard.*

We are often asked, what is the first thing you do or look for on a strange lake? Or even, where do you start on a lake you've never fished before? One really easy place to start is to turn over a few rocks around the launch ramp and check the color of the crawfish. Another is to simply drive around in the boat while your partner is parking the truck and see how deep the shad or baitfish are on your fish finder. Now you know what color your lures should be and how deep to fish.

But what's the first thing we do when we approach God? Today's verse tells us the first thing to do to have almighty God pay close attention to us: humble ourselves before God. Today, let's be humble before God and set our hearts completely on Him. I believe blessings will follow.

**TIP**
Heavy deepwater structures usually hold bluegill, crappie, and huge bass.

LUKE 12:31

*"Seek the kingdom of God, and all these things shall be added to you."*

In simple terms, if we want to find the fish we are seeking, we need to concentrate on what the fish are seeking. That is food, cover, safety, and comfortable water to call home. The game of catching them becomes much simpler when we apply this principle.

We're really not so different from fish in those ways; we need some of those same things. In today's verse Jesus was talking and teaching us how easy it is to have what we need in life—food, clothing, peace from worry. Seek God first! When? All the time and in everything we do. This is how we put God first in our lives—doing our best to honor Him in all we do. God is a rewarder. He loves to bless. Give it a try today and see what happens. Better yet, make it a habit.

**TIP**

Switch to heavier line if a crankbait is going too deep and picking up grass or debris.

JOHN 14:1

*"Let not your heart be troubled; you believe
in God, believe also in Me."*

With many bass spawned and yet some still heavily involved in the spawning process, late spring or early summer is the perfect time to fish a popping-type topwater bait. One of the keys to catching fish on this bait it to be sure and let the bait sit a few seconds before moving. The longer it sits, the more worried the bass gets. When it moves—*bam!*

In today's verse, Jesus was talking about worry and eternity. He was about to be crucified, yet was giving emotional and spiritual support to His disciples. This is the same support that is available to us today through Jesus. Jesus went on to tell them He was going to heaven to prepare a place for them—and for you and me. Do you have anxiety, problems, worry? Believe in Jesus; He can handle it, and will.

> **TIP**
> When all else fails, hit the tail end of every little pocket you can find. Use spinnerbaits and square-bills.

JEREMIAH 33:3

*"Call to Me, and I will answer you, and*
*show you great and mighty things."*

F allen logs are just about perfect structure for fishing a
spinnerbait. Most logs have several key junction areas
you can bring a spinnerbait by with
an excellent chance of getting a
strike. One is right where the log meets
the bank, another is where a limb meets the
main log, and of course the tip end of the
log. Often, I'll stop to fish a single log and
will return to it on future fishing trips.

To catch bass on logs, we need to
concentrate on junction areas. To receive
mighty things from God, we need merely
to call on Him. Jeremiah was in prison
when God gave him the promise in today's verse. Things
were bad and looking worse. When you face problems
and dire circumstances, call on God, stand back, and
watch the mighty happen! We serve a God who doesn't
consider the odds. He makes the odds. No army, no
prison, no problem is too big.

**TIP**

Trolling is
always an easy
way to locate
and catch fish.

ROMANS 3:23

*All have sinned and fall short of the glory of God.*

I've heard it a million times—we all have: "Don't catch 'em all." However, when Carl Lowrance invented the "little green box," the first depth finder ever, I told my dad, "Now I will catch them all!" Of course, I never did. Even now, with the amazing advances in electronics, I still can't catch 'em all—even though we can see and identify each individual fish.

But God, sure enough, has caught us all sinning. That's right; each and every single one of us. He is watching right now and will witness every sin we commit today. What hope do we have? Well, none without Jesus. But with Jesus, we have all the hope in the world. No matter what sins we committed in the past, commit today, or tomorrow, Jesus will cover and has covered these sins for us.

**TIP**

Try a white frog early in the morning during a shad spawn.

ROMANS 3:24

*. . . being justified freely by His grace through*
*the redemption that is in Christ Jesus.*

It is no secret that Chris and I helped pay our way through college selling catfish. We caught them on trotlines and on rod and reel. One of the very best places to fish for catfish with a rod and reel is under schooling, spawning gar. If you can find a flat in fifteen-to-twenty-foot water with gar rolling on top, almost certainly there will be catfish feeding below them on the bottom. Get that skillet ready!

It is ironic that we use what is considered by many as trash fish (gar) to catch one of America's favorite eating fish (catfish). When God looks at mankind, He sees an evil, perverse, sinful people. But through His perfect Son, Jesus, and His amazing grace, we are redeemed and justified before an almighty God forever. Now, that's grace. God's grace is available right now.

**TIP**
Roland Martin's favorite bladed jig technique is to let it fall to the bottom and slow roll it back in.

DEUTERONOMY 15:6

*The LORD your God will bless you just as He promised you.*

It is a real thrill to take someone fishing who absolutely gets a kick out of catching a fish and is just as happy and excited about the next one and the next! I recently fished with my friend Brad Martin and his son, Wesley. Wesley got so excited and laughed so much it had us all laughing and having more fun on every bass. His joy was not only a huge blessing for him but maybe even more to his dad and me. Awesome!

Blessings will come just as today's verse says, and they will come in all shapes, sizes, and forms. Many times, you are intended by God to be that blessing. Wesley was simply having fun catching bass and laughing; but what a blessing that became to us. Today, God will put in your path many opportunities to be a blessing. Try not to miss any of those opportunities.

**TIP**
Look for out-of-the-way places to fish.

# MAY 15

1 THESSALONIANS 5:18

*In everything give thanks; for this is the will*
*of God in Christ Jesus for you.*

It is really easy for a Christian to give thanks to God during the good times. Even non-Christians do it. This is especially true for many tournament fishermen. They stand on the stage and thank everyone, mostly sponsors, and they do usually include God and family. But how about the bad times? Terrible tournaments? Losing sponsors? Breakdowns? Illness? Total failure? What happens then? I believe these are the times we need to thank God the most.

Thanking God is one of the ways we fire ourselves up to get through a difficulty and whatever caused it. We are changing our focus from the problem to the Problem Solver. We have so many things to thank God for that the bad will begin to become less important—and maybe more important, you are doing the will of God. Then you know victory is on the way.

**TIP**

When fishing the shoreline, turn around frequently and make casts behind you.

JOB 12:12

*Wisdom is with aged men, and with length of days, understanding.*

I remember fishing a bass tournament on Lake Eufaula in Oklahoma back around 1970. My first-day partner draw in that tournament was Peewee Wadsworth. He didn't have his name written on his boat where it should have been. It simply said, "The Old Pro." Needless to say, I learned that day! We took my boat and fished my spots where I was catching plenty on a spinnerbait. He immediately started catching bass on a small crankbait. He said, "Jimmy, you need to throw a crankbait when the water is falling."

**TIP**
Isolated docks will normally produce better.

I made the top twenty in that event and collected a good check. But what I learned from fishing with "The Old Pro" was far more valuable. In the same way, it is smart to spend good quality time with older Christians in your family and in your church. When you see what God has done in their lives, it will strengthen your relationship with Him.

JAMES 1:5

*If any of you lacks wisdom, let him ask of God, who gives to all liberally and without reproach, and it will be given to him.*

Fishing knowledge and wisdom are readily available in today's world. We have literally thousands of fishing television shows, YouTube and Facebook videos, fishing seminars, and now even college courses in fishing. Guys and gals learning to fish can get expert information without even going near the water. But the real wisdom, knowledge, and skills can only be mastered with time on the water. Plus, that's where the fun begins!

In today's verse, James was not speaking of wisdom or knowledge gained in school. He was talking about wisdom to live a life according to God's will. To be at peace with God. To live righteously before men and almighty God. This kind of godly wisdom is what allows us to be happy, at peace, and full of joy. The best part is that all we need to do to get this wisdom is ask.

**TIP**
About 90 percent of the fish are in 10 percent of the water.

2 SAMUEL 22:21

*The LORD rewarded me according to my righteousness;*
*according to the cleanness of my hands.*

We love to take our kids and grandkids fishing. I'm often asked about my best memories in fishing. Most expect an answer about a particular tournament win or an Angler of the Year title. Those are cool and incredibly special. But my mind immediately goes to fishing memories with my kids and grandkids. I recall one instance with my daughter, Sherri, at about twelve or thirteen years old, catching a huge seven-pound-plus bass, and my son, Jamie, pushing me in the lake while filming on my fortieth birthday.

**TIP**
Always fish your best spots on major and minor phases of the moon, when fish are feeding.

Those memories are rewards from God. God's desire is to reward, to bless, to favor His children—you and me. Some may disagree, but I believe God rewards us for the way we live. As we read in today's verse, when we honor God by doing what is right and righteous in His eyes, He rewards. Let's live right with God today and see what God does next.

JOHN 14:14

*"If you ask anything in My name, I will do it."*

How many times have you asked God for another fish? If you are a tournament fisherman—even if you're not a Christian—it's a bunch. How about better health? A spouse? More money? Less pain? A better job? Hey, this list could go on forever—and I'm one of the many asking for God's help too! And, yes, God can and does supply all these things and more according to our needs and His will.

Jesus spoke the words in today's verse to His closest friends shortly before He was crucified, and He was telling them how to do His work on earth without Him being present. If they asked God in Jesus' name, they would have the power to do the same miracles He was performing and even greater works (John 14:12). Our prayers should be for things that glorify God, advance His kingdom, and make us better for His glory.

**TIP**

Use bluegill-colored baits after the bass spawn, as bluegill take over spawning areas.

COLOSSIANS 3:12

*As the elect of God, holy and beloved, put on tender*
*mercies, kindness, humility, meekness, longsuffering.*

People who fish want several different qualities in a fishing rod. What they are depends on what type of fishing you're doing, the size of the fish, and how you're catching them. Length, action, and weight are all important. Most of us also want a good-looking rod. Being pretty is important. But the really big deal is how it fishes—how it feels in your hands. The qualities the rod should exhibit all come down to personal preference.

Here, Paul was telling Christians in Colossus, those chosen by God, what qualities they should exhibit in their own personal lives. We must have compassion for others. God wants us to be good to them. He asks us to be humble and not be lovers of self. Being meek? That's a hard one! Yep, it means turning the other cheek when wronged. And be patient. These qualities make us feel good in God's hands.

**TIP**
Changing casting angles will sometimes trigger a strike—often a big one.

### JAMES 4:8

*Draw near to God and He will draw near to you.*

I've said for years that most bass fishermen fish too far away from the fish. Most make casts that are too long and end up fishing water where they have only a small chance of getting a bite. A good rule of thumb is, the heavier the cover, the closer you can fish to the bass. The clearer the water, the calmer the water, the less cover, the more we need to move back and make longer casts. Keep this in mind to catch more fish.

But can you come too close to God? I think not! How close can we get to almighty God? So close that God puts His Holy Spirit in us to lead and guide us in everything we do. Our job is to get as close to Him as we can. We do this by being in God's Word and by talking to Him.

**TIP**

Try letting a lipless crankbait fall to the bottom and rip it off the bottom to trigger strikes.

PSALM 138:8

*The LORD will perfect that which concerns me.*

Probably the best and most perfect bait to throw early in the year in the South is an umbrella rig (Alabama rig), especially in clearer water (but it's also productive in dingy water). When the bass are biting the umbrella rig, an A-rig can't be beat. We have caught so many big bass on this bait, it's amazing. It's so perfect it's not allowed in the top-level tournaments. I like the five bait rig with three-to-five-inch swimbaits in shad color.

In today's verse, David was praying to a God he knew could make perfect whatever problem he encountered—whatever situation with an enemy, whatever concern. And God did. God loved David, a man after His own heart, and God loves you and me. God will make perfect whatever concerns us as well. He's busy right now, perfecting your family, your job, your health, your career. Give your concerns to God today. Watch God in action.

**TIP**
Adding an oily scent to a jig head will allow it to slide inside a tube easier.

1 TIMOTHY 6:6

*Godliness with contentment is great gain.*

We are asked a lot about trailers on spinnerbaits, like soft plastics or pork. I prefer fishing a spinnerbait without a trailer because the trailer will hurt anyone's accuracy with this bait. We must be content to trade accuracy for more hookups. My key to adding a trailer is this: if I start missing fish, I add a trailer. Normally, a simple twin tail trailer in white or chartreuse will solve the problem. Being content with your fishing lure is often more difficult than being content in life.

In today's verse, Paul was reminding Timothy to be content with what he had. All he really needed was food and clothing. Most of us here in America take food and clothing for granted and aren't happy unless we have whatever else our hearts desire. These desires can lead us into destruction. I believe it is imperative to be content to please God and to be the people God wants us to be.

**TIP**

Ned rigs (small jig and worm) work well as a search bait because they cover water pretty quickly.

PSALM 63:1
*O God, You are my God; early will I seek You.*

We all know how much fun fishing can be early and late. The first two hours after daybreak and the last hour or two before dark can be magic. This is generally the best fishing all year. One reason is bass feed at night a lot, and these hours are close to nighttime. Maybe a more important reason is low light. Remember, cloud cover, rain, and wind also create these low light conditions and usually result in better fishing.

Do we need to pray early as well? Sure. I can tell you most tournament fishermen do. I sure did. We should want to get with God to start our days and continue this visit through-out each day. And when we end each day, let's rejoice and praise God for helping us through another day with Him. Today, thank God for His love.

**TIP**

After a cold front, try crawling a bladed jig (ChatterBait) through the grass or rocks on the bottom— really slow!

HEBREWS 10:22

*Let us draw near with a true heart in full assurance*
*of faith, having our hearts sprinkled from an evil*
*conscience and our bodies washed with pure water.*

As we move from late spring into summer, we need to be thinking about changes in our fishing. As the water clears, lighter line and smaller lures might be more productive. We may need to start looking a little deeper for the fish. Vegetation is growing, and this changes much of the structure we are fishing. As conditions evolve, our confidence may waver a bit.

Our confidence in God need never waver. Our faith should be full and rock-solid. Our guilty conscience from past sins should be clean. Jesus has washed us with His grace. Whatever we need, whatever our problem, we can confidently take it to the throne of God. God's love for us is so great, His faithfulness so full, that He will always reward us for our faith and confidence in Him.

**TIP**

Learn to cast adequately both left-handed and right-handed for emergencies.

JIMMY HOUSTON

MICAH 7:8

*Do not rejoice over me, my enemy; when I fall, I will arise; when I sit in darkness, the LORD will be a light to me.*

It seems that anytime a big-time tournament fisherman or television fisherman makes a mistake or is even accused of making one, lots of folks start piling on. On YouTube and Facebook, we call them trolls. Unfortunately, this happens in everyday life as well. And the bigger you are, the more successful, the more popular, the happier, kinder, more righteous—the more they pile on. My buddy Hank Parker once told me, "People will forgive you of anything but success."

Micah was God's messenger to tell Judah of God's judgment for their sins and idolatry. As you can see in today's scripture, Micah's enemies rejoiced over his difficulties. Yet despite his dire predictions that came true, Micah was so positive, so upbeat, because of his trust in his Lord. Whatever your enemy, you, too, will rise. You will shine in the Lord's light.

**TIP**

Increase sensitivity and feel on crankbaits with braided line tied directly to the bait— no leader.

GALATIANS 5:25

*If we live in the Spirit, let us also walk in the Spirit.*

At the first Bass 'n Gal Tournament ever on Toledo Bend Lake, I was asked to be the weighmaster. As we came closer to the end of this competition, it became apparent that only a few women had a chance to win. One was my wife, Chris. As I placed her bag of bass on the scales, they settled in one ounce short; I could have called the weight a few ounces more and Chris would have won. But I didn't, and she lost by one ounce.

Today's scripture is easy for us to understand but difficult to put into practice. In practical terms, we walk the talk. We listen, listen, listen to what the Holy Spirit is telling us and then put it into practice day by day. We live in love, joy, peace, goodness, self-control, patience, and gentleness. We get rid of lying, adultery, envy, anger, hatred, and more. Get the picture? Let's start our walk in the Spirit, no matter what the temptation to cut corners may be.

> **TIP**
>
> My favorite weight for flipping jigs in heavy cover is a half-ounce Luck-E-Strike jig. Most will bite on the initial drop.

PHILIPPIANS 4:11

*I have learned in whatever state I am, to be content.*

Fishing is a bit like bowling. You can't throw a strike every time, and you sure can't make a perfect cast every time. A sure way to become a better fisherman is to learn to make better casts, flip better, and pitch better. Obviously, the more you fish, the better caster you will become. But when you're not fishing, practice, practice, practice. I recommend keeping a rod and target in your living room. Practice pitching and flipping a bit every day, and you'll be more content with your skills.

Learning to be content in life is far more important, and it's also much more difficult. It's hard because the devil doesn't want you to be content, happy, healthy, or successful. He's constantly attacking your mind with negative ideas. Fight that by knowing God is always with you and working on your behalf. Wherever you are is perfect with God there.

**TIP**
Use your side scan sonar to slowly scan the bank before you fish it. This will show you the best structures to fish.

JAMES 1:19
*My beloved brethren, let every man be swift*
*to hear, slow to speak, slow to wrath.*

A jig can be fished in so many different ways; it's a versatile bait. My buddy Tommy Monsoor is maybe the best swim jig fisherman ever, and he's certainly been my teacher. One of his keys to swim jig fishing is to use fewer strands in the jig for better action. And another is, "Don't set the hook!" Simply start winding faster, he says, when you get a bite. You will miss fewer fish. I always value Tommy's advice.

Today's verse is even more important advice. If every man and woman, as today's verse says, would follow God's advice to be swift to hear, slow to speak, and slow to wrath, what a wonderful world this would be. The fact is, you and I can. And we should because of what God has done for us. Let's make this our goal today.

**TIP**
A jerkbait will often catch the largest fish when bass are schooling.

HEBREWS 3:7

*Therefore, as the Holy Spirit says: "Today, if you will hear His voice . . ."*

Payne Stewart was one of the greatest golf pros ever. He was a dear friend, a wonderful Christian man, and a really skilled fisherman. We were fishing a tournament together as partners in Florida and whackin' 'em on a blue-and-chrome lipless crankbait. I hooked a nice four-pound bass. Seeing it was really hooked, I simply swung it into the boat. While I was unhooking her, Stewart hooked her identical twin! Seeing his bass was barely hooked, I hollered, "Don't swing it, don't swing it!" He heard me but didn't listen and lost that bass. We finished second place, and that lost bass cost us the win.

Today God's Holy Spirit will be speaking to you. Listen. Pay attention. Follow His advice. God created you to win and will always guide and lead you every day to victory.

**TIP**
On holiday weekends, when lakes are super crowded, concentrate your time in No Wake Zone areas. Some are behind marinas.

CATCH A BETTER LIFE

1 JOHN 2:17

*The world is passing away, and the lust of it; but*
*he who does the will of God abides forever.*

Once we begin a tournament day, stop our boat, and make that first cast, we are closer to the end of that tournament. We have plenty of time to make that day special and receive the rewards of a well-fished tournament. But quickly that day comes to an end; it passes away.

God says this world is passing away. It could happen today or years from now. That day is in God's time, His decision. Doing His will is believing in His Son, Jesus, repenting of our sins, and making Him Lord of our lives. This guarantees we will be with God forever in heaven. Just as we fish and make every second of that tournament day count, we make every day count for God in this lustful, evil world. Jesus in our lives makes each day better and much happier for us and those around us.

**TIP**
Wake a spinnerbait around flooded timber in high water.

JUNE

## JUNE 1

PROVERBS 3:27
*Do not withhold good from those to whom it is due.*

Teaching folks to fish can really be frustrating for fishing pros. We see the same mistakes made over and over, some of which we haven't made in years. Many times, we're teaching our own kids or spouses or friends. The key to our success and theirs is to dwell on the good and not the bad. This is definitely not easy. Just remember, it's scriptural. Praise them for the good they do, and bite your tongue on the bad. It makes for a much better fishing trip.

As you can see from today's scripture, this is also how God asks us to be good neighbors, good friends, and helpers to those we come in contact with. Anytime we have the opportunity and ability to help someone, God says we should (Galatians 6:10). God blesses us with talents, abilities, time, and resources so we can use them to bless others. Let's do good to someone today!

**TIP**
Small, bluegill-colored popping topwaters produce after bass spawn.

PHILIPPIANS 2:14
*Do all things without complaining and disputing.*

Get a bunch of fishermen together and throw a subject out there to see what happens. Maybe the best way to fish a spinnerbait, or how best to catch fish after a cold front. Here's a good one: Who makes the best boat electronics, outboard motor, reels, lures? Some complaining and surely a bunch of disputes are about to happen. This is not all bad because if you will keep quiet, you will probably learn something!

But complaining and disputing are not how God wants us to live our lives. My dad once told me to never complain. He said, "Half the people you are complaining to don't care; the other half are glad you have a problem!" We know that kids are the worst at complaining. But how often do all of us carry this childish behavior into our everyday conversations? Today, every time a complaining or disruptive thought pops into your head, try to zip it up and not say it.

**TIP**
Watch for freshly spawned bass fry in treetops.

ISAIAH 30:21

*Your ears shall hear a word behind you,*
*saying, "This is the way, walk in it."*

One of the best things about little rules of thumb in fishing is they will pop into your mind at just the right time. You just need to listen. If it starts raining, immediately I think the fish start looking up, and it's a perfect time to fish a spinnerbait or buzzbait. More often than not, it works. And this list of rules of thumb goes on and on.

In today's scripture, God assured Isaiah that He would always be there with him; Isaiah just needed to listen to know what to do. When we get saved, God gives us His Holy Spirit to be with us at all times and guide us. The way I see it, that's how God communicates with millions at the same time. It's better than Facebook and YouTube! We need to listen and walk in God's way.

**TIP**

Throw crankbaits when the water is falling.

JIMMY HOUSTON

EPHESIANS 4:31

*Let all bitterness, wrath, anger, clamor, and evil*
*speaking be put away from you, with all malice.*

R ay Murski was one of the early pro tournament fishermen. Ray was mostly a worm guy, and worm fishing
was done a little differently in the early days. In tournaments, he had a habit of completely losing his cool
when he missed or lost a fish. When
that happened, you knew it from several
hundred yards away!

Today's scripture directs us to put away
anger and evil speaking. Why does God say
these words and feelings are bad? I believe
it's because they steal our joy. All these are
directed at someone else, but we are often
the ones suffering from these words and
attitudes. Many times, the other person has
long since forgotten the incident but we are
still bitter or angry. Let's pray for God's help
to get bad feelings and habits out of our
hearts and minds today.

**TIP**
Fish have no
hands, so when
you feel a bite,
set the hook,
and you'll know
it is in the
fish's mouth.

# JUNE 5

## 1 CORINTHIANS 15:33

*Do not be deceived: "Evil company corrupts good habits."*

It's no secret that Roland Martin, over the years, has taught me a lot about fishing. One key piece of advice from years ago was to get in the good habit of always keeping one eye on your fish finder at all times. He taught me that looking away even for just a few seconds could be costly. With today's advanced electronics, I can hardly take my eyes off of them.

We all need good habits, but we know it's often a challenge to keep them intact. Just think about how hard it is to maintain good eating habits. I suspect we all have friends who are not saved, friends who are not righteous, maybe even evil. I believe Paul was telling us here that they may change us. Either our good habits will change them, or their evil company will change us. Just maybe we need to examine who we are running around with.

**TIP**

Use a gold or fire tiger lipless crankbait or Mimic in dirty or dingy water.

ROMANS 6:23

*The wages of sin is death, but the gift of God is*
*eternal life in Christ Jesus our Lord.*

Saltwater fishing can be totally different from
fishing freshwater. Chris and I had never
even seen saltwater until after we got out
of college. When we got our first chance at
fishing saltwater, we couldn't believe how
such a small fish could fight so hard. It made
me want to add salt to my drinking water.
What a difference in the fish!

The difference between sin and righteousness is enormous—much bigger than
salt water and fresh water. It's life and death.
We all sin, and sin leads us to separation
from God here on earth during this life and
for eternity when we die. God's gift is Jesus,
who gave His blood as the payment for our
sins. Accept this gift from God, and live life here better
today and forever with Jesus Christ in heaven.

**TIP**

If you have kids
or grandkids,
let them catch
crawfish
with bacon.

## JUNE 7

**LUKE 10:18**

*[Jesus] said to them, "I saw Satan fall like lightning from heaven."*

It's exciting anytime we witness a feeding frenzy while fishing, when the fish are really turned on and will strike just about anything that comes close. We keep a fish feeder on our pier at the Eagle, and it's always fun to turn that feeder on for a spin every time we get on that pier. It's just special to watch the commotion of hundreds of bluegill attacking that fish food.

Can you imagine what it was like when the devil rebelled against God and was kicked out of heaven? What a commotion when Satan tried to become God! He failed, and, with a third of the angels, was hurled to earth. This same devil and his band of demon angels want to inhabit your life. Don't let them in. They are here to destroy. They use lies, gossip, envy, strife, malice, filthy language, alcohol, drugs, whatever it takes. Be on guard; don't let them in.

**TIP**

Bass like to build spawning beds underneath willow bushes.

PROVERBS 8:18

*Riches and honor are with me, enduring riches and righteousness.*

We teach kids about fishing because it's such a wholesome sport. It's done outdoors, where they can easily have fun. Fishing doesn't require super physical skills or athletic ability in order to take part. And it's readily available pretty much everywhere. It's a sport they can enjoy the rest of their lives.

Today's proverb unlocks the keys to some other important rewards you can enjoy in your older years: prosperity, honor, and righteousness. That means we need to live our lives now with wisdom, prudence, knowledge, and discretion, and we gain these by honoring God in all we do. This wisdom is godly wisdom given to us as we grow with Him. It's not immediate and doesn't happen overnight, just as you can't learn all you need to know about fishing in one trip. Ask God for more wisdom every day. Enduring riches and righteousness will be your rewards.

**TIP**

Black licorice on a hook is a good bait for kids to use while fishing, plus they can eat what's left.

HEBREWS 10:35

*Do not cast away your confidence, which has great reward.*

What is your confidence bait? What do you believe in when it's tough to get a bite? Although I prefer spinnerbaits, as I've mentioned earlier, the best bait tends to be a moving target depending on what the water is doing, the time of year, type of lake, and weather. I do think it's good to spend 20 percent of every fishing day using baits you have little or no practice with or affinity for. Learning to fish these baits well will give you confidence.

In today's verse, Paul was telling the Hebrew Christians and us to never lose the confidence we have in God's saving grace. Our trust is in Jesus, and we have an endurance race to run here on earth. We will face trials and tribulations. We will be chastised and even persecuted at times. We will fail at times, but we must keep our faith in Christ Jesus. Our reward is eternal life in heaven!

**TIP**

Catfish can survive and thrive in small pieces of water, like creeks, or almost no water at all; don't overlook them.

GALATIANS 6:10

*As we have opportunity, let us do good to all.*

One of the very best places to fish is around bridges. You have bridge pilings, riprap, channels, and points all in one nice little location. I've fished entire tournaments and cashed good checks on a single bridge or two. What's really cool is you can fish them from the bank without a boat. It's a smart plan to know every bridge around where you live. It's also good to carry a rod or two in your car or truck to check these bridges out when you have the opportunity.

In today's verse, Paul was telling us to help folks every time we can. Not just occasionally, but continually look for these opportunities. For us as true believers this is not a burden; it's a privilege—especially when we help other Christians. Keep an eye out for those nearby bridges to fish. While you're there, God just might provide you with someone to help!

**TIP**

Believe you are going to catch a fish on the very next cast.

1 PETER 2:4

*Coming to [Jesus] as to a living stone, rejected indeed*
*by men, but chosen by God and precious . . .*

When I won my first Oklahoma State Championship as a senior in college, Chris and I were living day by day and loving every minute. We had a precious two-year-old baby girl, and we were working sixty to seventy hours a week each to pay for our college educations. But we were still fishing. I took a week off work to practice fish for that tournament. We had little money. I ate bologna sandwiches and slept on a concrete picnic table in the park near the boat ramp so I could fish from daybreak until dark.

I know how hard a concrete picnic table is, but it's nothing in comparison to the "living stone" in today's scripture: Jesus. I know how solid the Jesus I've trusted my eternity to is! Peter called Him precious and chosen by God. That makes you and me precious to God as well if we belong to Jesus.

**TIP**
Search out isolated grass patches in open flats.

REVELATION 1:7

*Behold, He is coming with clouds, and every eye*
*will see Him, even they who pierced Him.*

Sight fishing during spawning season is extremely exciting. It's exciting because we see so many large female bass swimming around. It's exciting when the bass of a lifetime takes your bait. It's exciting to see all these giant bass. And it's exciting to know more of these fantastic fish are being created.

Think about the commotion around the world when Jesus comes back. Huge stadiums packed with people will be nothing compared to Christ's return. All over the world, some will be saying, "What's that?" "Who's that?" We'll tell them, "It's Jesus, and He told us He was coming." As today's scripture tells us, "Every eye will see Him," in Australia, Russia, Africa, China—everywhere. Tens of thousands of angels will appear and watch this glorious, heavenly entry. Everyone who has ever died will rise and see, even the ones who hung Jesus on the cross. Now, that's exciting!

**TIP**
Fishing with different people will increase your fishing skill.

JOEL 2:32

*It shall come to pass that whoever calls on the
name of the Lord shall be saved.*

Sounds are important in fishing. Many times, a fish
will give away its location by moving in the water and
striking bait. I can't hear nearly as
well now as when I was younger;
I used to be able to hear a minnow eat a
gnat at a hundred yards! But sound is still a
major factor to me in fishing. A good rule
of thumb is to throw at any movement or
sound in the water. It could be something
you really want to catch.

That sound you are hearing, if you are
not saved, is Jesus knocking on the door of
your heart. If you are saved, it might be His
Holy Spirit calling on you to live closer to Him. Whatever
it is, call out to Him today, repent of your sins, ask Jesus
to save you, and make Him Lord of your life—and you
will be saved.

**TIP**
Fish flooded
yards in
extremely high
water with a
buzzbait.

PSALM 113:7

*He raises the poor out of the dust, and lifts the needy out of the ash heap.*

This time of the year, the players begin to take over our lakes—water skiers, tubers, Jet Skis, power boats. The solution is to rise early to go fishing. It's topwater time, especially during those first couple of hours of calm, dead slick water. We can raise a bass from pretty deep. Fish slowly and deliberately. You might want to break out that fly rod and catch some big bluegill. This might turn a poor fishing day into a fun one!

God raises us up too, no matter how deep the water we're in. Our God is so powerful that He must actually humble Himself to look at us. But He loves us so much that He does. He cares about our circumstances and corrects them. As you can see from today's scripture, we serve a God who also cares about our financial situations. Put any money problems you might have in God's hands. Rest assured, He can turn them into abundance.

> **TIP**
> Pay close attention to changes in the wind or cloud cover.

PROVERBS 19:11
*The discretion of a man makes him slow to anger,*
*and his glory is to overlook a transgression.*

We call the very best places to fish "honey holes." We are always looking for these special spots. How do you go about finding some of these on your own? One of the easiest ways is to find shallow water cover and fish close to a deepwater-type spot, such as a point, a bend in a creek, or a hump. Find these spots, and you may have found a honey hole!

TIP
Parallel the banks to cover water more efficiently and catch more fish.

To find a man or woman who has glory from God, look for these two qualities: being slow to anger and being forgiving. It seems to me these are two of the many superb qualities of our Lord and Savior, Jesus Christ. As we go through today, this week, I'm fairly sure you and I will get a chance to emulate Jesus in these areas. Let's make sure to do it.

1 CORINTHIANS 16:2

*On the first day of the week let each one of you lay*
*something aside, storing up as he may prosper.*

To become good at anything, you must put much effort and time into becoming better. Casting proficiently is no different. If you spend more time practicing casting, pitching, and flipping, your effort will be rewarded with more and larger fish. The benefits far outweigh the practice time.

Tithing, also, is an attribute where the benefits outweigh the effort, or the tithe. As I've been told, tithing is not mentioned as a set amount in the New Testament. That is true. But I'm a believer in tithing. I believe a tithe to God is 10 percent, and an offering is that amount above 10 percent you want to give. Whatever you give to God and His work, God will bless you. And you cannot outgive God! Unlike casting, we don't tithe to be rewarded; we tithe to honor God. But this I know: when I honor God, amazing things happen.

**TIP**

On windy days, go to a half-ounce spinnerbait with a single number four or number five blade.

JAMES 1:2–3

*My brethren, count it all joy when you fall into various trials,*
*knowing that the testing of your faith produces patience.*

It is true that one little clue, one strike, one idea, can completely change any fishing day in tournament fishing. It has happened to me many times, both in tournament practice and on actual competition days. This is why we practice daylight till dark on those allowed practice days.

It's exactly the same in everyday life. We never know what might unlock a major blessing or event in our lives. That one thing is often a trial or test or hurdle we must overcome. It's kind of like fighting through stumps, shallow water, or brush to get back into a honey hole that very few find. God is always working on our behalf and wants us to be happy, content, and joyful while we are going through these trials. Patience and honey holes are on the way!

**TIP**
Use a LiveScope to locate underwater stumps in two to six feet of water.

1 PETER 4:8

*Above all things have fervent love for one another,*
*for "love will cover a multitude of sins."*

Spotted bass, or Kentucky bass as they are often called, are eating machines. Nothing dominates their life above food. Most of our southern lakes have spotted bass, and, in good shad years, these rascals become butterballs! Some California lakes also produce unbelievably big spotted bass that dominate the water.

Since we are Christians, love should dominate all aspects of our lives—even more than that bass loves food. This love needs to be put into practice; it's not just an emotion. We help folks. We speak pleasantly to everyone, even strangers and enemies. The last part of today's verse is the tough part: "love will cover a multitude of sins." This means we must forgive. Be ready today. Just like that spotted bass finding food, you'll find an opportunity to overlook sins and forgive someone today through love. It happens all the time!

**TIP**
Drag a Carolina rig with a simple stop-and-go method.

## JOHN 8:7

*"He who is without sin among you, let him throw a stone at her first."*

One of the most priceless times to be on the water is when it is dead calm. We make a cast and the ripples seem to travel forever. As magic as this calm is, it can really pose a problem. The fish know we are there. We need to fish with our trolling motors on low speeds. Do not bang anything down in the boat. Be very, very quiet. This can be more like hunting than fishing.

> **TIP**
> Always wait until you feel the fish to set the hook on topwater strikes.

Like noise on the quiet water, when we condemn others of sin, it can actually destroy the calm in our own lives, especially if we are guilty of that same sin. In today's scripture, religious leaders brought a woman to Jesus whom they'd caught committing adultery; they asked Him to confirm their plan to stone her to death. Jesus, knowing their sin, turned their own words against them. Today, our best bet might be to not condemn others!

JAMES 1:12

*Blessed is the man who endures temptation; for when he has been approved, he will receive the crown of life.*

This is the time of the year when bass, catfish, crappie, stripers, and similar fish have a wide variety of things to eat. Bluegill and shad are spawning. Bass and crappie are growing every day and provide lots of tasty fry. Crawfish are available. It is our job to figure out where they are eating and match our lures and lure colors to tempt these fish into biting.

The devil's job is to tempt us into sinning. Sin brings pain, destruction, and death. Sin steals our joy. As we read in today's scripture, we're blessed when we pass Satan's test of temptation. We pass this test by being faithful, by relying on God's strength, and by choosing our friends wisely. Let's be careful; there's a big, sharp hook in Satan's temptations. Let's avoid that hook and have a full, victorious life. Run, devil, run!

**TIP**
After bass spawn, they usually suspend two to six feet deep over deeper water—as deep as twenty feet or more.

# JUNE 21

GENESIS 27:35

*Your brother came with deceit and has taken away your blessing.*

Fishing is truly a game of deceit. We are trying to trick a fish into striking an artificial lure that looks like a free lunch, or we are using live bait or food the fish love. The deceit is, we have a hook in it.

Today's famous verse is about Esau's twin brother, Jacob, stealing away Esau's blessing by deceit. We can be like Esau and let others say things and do things that take away our blessings, such as discouraging us, running us down, or saying bad things about us. Or we can be like Jacob and say or do things that cost someone else his or her blessing. We can even do this unintentionally at times. I'm thinking we don't want to be either one of these brothers. First, don't let anyone talk you out of your blessings. Second, be very careful when saying something to or about anyone.

> **TIP**
>
> Mashing your barbs down when crappie fishing will save lots of baits without losing many fish.

EPHESIANS 5:18

*Do not be drunk with wine, in which is*
*dissipation; but be filled with the Spirit.*

No alcohol is allowed in our boats during practice or competition days in national bass tournaments. It was allowed in earlier tournaments. I don't drink, but I remember a B.A.S.S. tournament on Lake Seminole around 1970 when one partner broke out a bottle of whiskey about 9:00 a.m.! I think it was a quart or so. By midafternoon that bottle was empty, and so was his fishing ability. I stood very high in the tournament, on lots of fish! During the day he got twenty-six bites—that's right, twenty-six—and caught only *one* bass. That whiskey had totally dissipated his fishing skills.

**TIP**
Concentrate on single stickups when fishing post-spawn flats.

Scripture doesn't condemn drinking, but it does condemn drunkenness. It will dissipate your health, wealth, family, friends, job, and yes, even your fish catching. Instead, you can be filled with the Holy Spirit. What an awesome trade.

# JUNE 23

## JOHN 8:36

*"If the Son makes you free, you shall be free indeed."*

Catch-and-release bass fishing is a staple in today's tournament rules. When we started fishing, and even several years into our tournament career, keeping bass was the ticket. No one released them. For many years, on our television shows, we received hundreds of letters every year asking why we threw the bass back! Catch and release has definitely made bass fishing better. But can I tell you—it's okay to keep a few and eat 'em.

Fortunately, God practices catch and keep. Once we give our lives to Him and make Him Lord of our lives, He never lets go. But He does free us from past sins, bad habits, addictions, poor decisions, and other mistakes. He also frees us from some of the bad things that have been passed down to us from generation to generation. How wonderful to know that we are His always, and He's able to set us free!

> **TIP**
> Be sure to check your boat trailer wheel bearings occasionally.

1 PETER 3:12

*The eyes of the LORD are on the righteous, and*
*His ears are open to their prayers.*

Roland Martin talks about being a line watcher. He's talking about focusing on his line, watching for anything different—a little slack, a little jump, a little flash or swirl in the water—and setting the hook! That's becoming a lost art with our new electronics that we almost glue our eyes and attention to. But it's still just as important as ever.

God sees everything. He doesn't miss a thing, such as all the bad we do—but more important, all the good. Today's scripture tells us God is listening to the prayers of the righteous. Obviously, God listens to sinners' prayers; but to me, this means God is really paying attention when the righteous pray. Our job is to be righteous and bring a smile to God. The angel Gabriel once told Daniel, "The very moment you started praying, I was sent" (Daniel 9:23 CEV). I'll take that deal every day.

> **TIP**
> Flare your weedguard on a jig for more hookups and less hang-ups.

PSALM 8:6–8
*You have put all things under his feet . . . even the
beasts of the field . . . and the fish of the sea.*

God created the fish, the game, and the birds of the earth. He also gave us dominion over them. He gave us the ability to think, to figure out better ways to fish and hunt. For the most part, the fish don't know we are trying to catch them! Other animals do often learn they are on the hit list and avoid certain areas.

But more than giving us dominion over fish and game, God has put all things under our feet through Jesus Christ. We can put our feet on the neck of everything bad that tries to enter our lives, such as sickness, poor finances, toxic relationships, and job problems. God has given us victory in life and victory hereafter as well. Whatever you need dominion over, claim it in Jesus' name and get ready for God to do something special.

**TIP**
Add a swivel to a jigging spoon to avoid line twisting.

JIMMY HOUSTON

JOEL 2:28

*"It shall come to pass afterward that I will pour out My Spirit on all flesh."*

It's a thrill for fishermen to make their own lures and go out and catch fish on them. I'm sure early fishermen made these lures by necessity to catch dinner. Don Rawlins at Spike-It has developed a complete line of soft plastics, molds, and accessories that make this possible. This saves money and makes it fun to build a lure and whack 'em on it. It's really satisfying when you take a liquid and pour it into a mold to make it into a spectacular fish-catching bait.

This is something like what God does when we make Jesus Lord of our lives. He literally pours His Holy Spirit into us, and He's there to comfort us. He's there to lead us into better decision-making. God's Holy Spirit is always available to us, but only if we listen to Him. You have to rely on God's Spirit every day!

**TIP**

A spinnerbait and a bladed jig are our two most versatile baits year-round.

# JUNE 27

## MATTHEW 7:3

*"Why do you look at the speck in your brother's eye, but do not consider the plank in your own eye?"*

We all love fishing around brush. That's where lots of bass and crappie live. The more brush we fish, the more fish we will catch. But we need to learn how to fish brush without getting hung up much. We also need to learn how to unhang our baits. Learn the bow-and-arrow technique, where you hold the line in your hand and use the rod tip as the bow to power a big impact down the line and free the lure. This saves lots of baits!

We can get hung up in the weeds of life too, and we find ourselves in sin. Today's scripture challenges us to look at our own shortcomings instead of worrying about the small things wrong in others. People who focus on others' shortcomings and not their own are hypocrites—and there are plenty warming church pews. Today, when we see others' mistakes, let's just zip it up and check our own hang-ups.

**TIP**
Use hog pellets to attract catfish to summertime flats.

JOHN 6:31

*"He gave them bread from heaven to eat."*

Several times during Chris's twenty-plus wins on the Bass 'n Gal Tournament trail, the winning margin was razor-thin, from a few ounces to maybe just one fish. Sometimes a really big fish caught in the last few minutes of the tournament gave her the win. She coined the phrase, "The fish just fell out of heaven." Of course, she was recognizing the fish as a gift from God.

Today's verse is about God giving the Israelites manna to eat in the desert. I personally believe every good gift, like the manna, is a blessing from God. Why and how does this happen? I believe God drops gifts from heaven when we put Him first and honor Him with our lives. That's why He blesses us. Plus, He loves us so much. This is easy for God because He knows exactly what we need and when we need it. Here's the key to unlock it all: we must expect that heavenly blessing drop.

**TIP**
For a summertime break, try alligator gar fishing.

PROVERBS 28:25

*He who is of a proud heart stirs up strife, but he who trusts in the LORD will be prospered.*

Tournament fishing seems to be a spawning ground for pride. Let a fisherman win a tournament or two, or have a little hot streak finishing in the money, and "big head" is not just describing a carp. I've seen good guys become almost impossible to be around when they are winning. Is this something we should be concerned about? Can it hurt us?

God really dislikes pride, especially since we usually get a proud heart not from some super accomplishment but from some godly gifts, blessings, and victories from God. Plus, as you can see in today's verse, pride causes problems. It often stirs up feelings better left alone. It takes effort, but we have to bury pride and replace it with trust. Real trust allows God to prosper us; and if we are smart, we'll be humble about it.

**TIP**

Spike-It Dip-N-Glo Garlic is the number one scent attractant.

ACTS 23:1

*"Men and brethren, I have lived in all good*
*conscience before God until this day."*

Summertime fishing produces fewer really big bass than spring or even fall. Why is that? Well, the fish do weigh a little less after the spawn, but mainly it's a situation of availability. The big bass become less available. They have lived longer and been caught a time or two more. They position themselves in a little deeper water, move around a lot, are spookier, and can't be fooled as easily.

Bass may be cagey, but they have no conscience, as we do. And our consciences need to be clear before God, as Paul's was in today's verse. When we have those opportunities to fudge a little in life, we don't fudge. We don't tell that little lie that would help our situation. We don't repeat the gossip. We don't argue, even when we are right. When no one else is looking, God is. Let's try to keep our consciences in good standing today.

**TIP**

Be prepared to change techniques often when conditions change.

JULY

PSALM 55:22

*Cast your burden on the LORD, and He shall sustain you.*

"Match the hatch." I'm sure this is a phrase coined by a fly fisherman. They are very precise in matching their trout fly to exactly what the fish are eating. The very best fly fishermen are meticulous at this. We use the same philosophy with other fish. Give them what they are eating. Give them what they want. For bass you can usually use a little larger bait since they are big fish.

I can tell you, God wants your burdens, your problems, your shortcomings, just as much as a fish wants to eat. We talk to our earthly fathers to get help with our burdens. Our heavenly Father wants the same. What is your burden today? Give it to God. It will be the best cast you can make! Plus, it comes with a promise: God will sustain you through your burden.

**TIP**
Most shad have a little blue in them in the sunlight; so should your lure.

JOHN 20:22

*He breathed on them, and said to them, "Receive the Holy Spirit."*

I get kidded a lot about getting fish breath from kissing so many bass. But I've got to tell you, I want to smell like a fish after a day on the water! I want my boat, my clothes, my livewell, everything to smell like fish. That's proof positive of a wonderful day fishing. And it smells really good to me.

When we are saved, God breathes His Holy Spirit on us, and He is there permanently. This is God breathing favor on our lives—God breathing victory, instruction, well-being, wisdom, and understanding. When God breathes on us, He gives us gifts and abilities that He chose for us. One breath of God's Spirit will change our lives forever. If you haven't accepted that personal relationship with Jesus, do that right now. God will breathe His Spirit into your life.

**TIP**

Spotted bass love to suspend around submerged and visible treetops. The bass will kill topwater baits, spinnerbaits, and buzzbaits.

PROVERBS 25:28

*Whoever has no rule over his own spirit is like*
*a city broken down, without walls.*

S wimming a jig is all about control. You need to be able
to swim that jig at just the right depth and speed to
entice a bass to bite. One trick is to really pay attention to
both the contour on the bank above the water and your
fish finder. If you use a forward-looking transducer, it
makes swimming a jig that much easier and much more
productive, and you'll be able to control it
better.

**TIP**

The best swim
jigs have
little or no
weedguards.
Fish them
carefully
around brush.

Today's proverb is about controlling
our spirits, how we act in everyday life
situations. When we can't control our
tempers, our language, even our thinking,
we have no protection against evil—
against the devil. We are tempted more
easily to say or do something we will later
regret. To be successful, to be happy, to
be someone others want to be around, we
must control our spirits. I believe God will
honor us for that.

EPHESIANS 4:29

*Let no corrupt word proceed out of your mouth,*
*but what is good for necessary edification.*

E ven a fish wouldn't get into trouble if it didn't open its
mouth! We trick them into biting by placing something nice and attractive in front of them. Ugly baits
might attract and catch fish, but I know fishermen who
are not too attracted to ugly baits.

We don't like ugly baits, and we
definitely don't like ugly words about
us, but what about our words, our
language? As you can see from today's verse,
Christians should never use bad words, even
when we get a backlash or lose a personal
best. And yes, I'm talking to myself here.
But more important, we must speak words
that encourage, that instruct, that lift others
up. Let's make this our goal and see how
others and God react.

**TIP**

Move to heavy
tungsten
weights (one
and a half
ounce and
up) to punch
thick mats.

## JULY 5

GALATIANS 6:9
*Let us not grow weary while doing good, for in due*
*season we shall reap if we do not lose heart.*

Tournament practice is brutal. It takes three full days,
from daylight to dark, in all sorts of conditions.
Other things about fishing are hard too, like learning to
flip or pitch accurately. How about
walking the dog with a Luck-E-
Dog, slow rolling a spinnerbait, or
learning how to use a trailer hook without
hanging up too much? All these take time,
patience, and, yes, practice. But do all this
and you will reap more and bigger bass.

Doing good is hard too. Many times it
feels like a kick in the head. Often the very
ones we help don't even say thank you. This
happened to Jesus Himself when he healed
ten men with leprosy. Only one came back
to thank and praise Jesus. Let's do what today's verse says:
keep doing good, be happy, and get ready to reap.

**TIP**
After the
spawn, bass
move to the
outside edges
of the grass.

2 CHRONICLES 14:7

*"We have sought the LORD our God . . . and He has given us rest on every side." So they built and prospered.*

One of the best lakes to fish in Oklahoma during the summer is Lake Eufaula. It is one of the largest lakes in the world. Parts of this giant lake are simply too muddy to catch much in the spring, but the water becomes a stable fish-catching color in the summertime. All parts of the South have these muddy lakes, rivers, and creeks. Seek these places out in the summer and fall for terrific fishing.

**TIP**
Search out major creek ends and creeks running into rivers during late-summer drought conditions.

As we read in today's scripture, when we seek God, He will prosper us. We need to seek Him every day, in all situations, and do so with all our hearts. The more we seek and include God, the more He helps. We make better decisions and we prosper. As a bonus, God gives us rest from our enemies, even the devil.

PSALM 89:16
*In Your name they rejoice all day long, and in*
*Your righteousness, they are exalted.*

It's not necessary to be an athlete to enjoy fishing. It is true, tournament fishing does take lots of athletic ability. Fishing all day standing up takes a lot of stamina. It might help some to be younger, but I had a rather good year last year!

We don't need stamina, athletic ability, or youth to rejoice all day in God's awesome name. All we need is a relationship with the God who hung the moon and stars. The closer we are to Him, the more we have to rejoice about. That relationship also makes us totally righteous. The bonus: we will be exalted by almighty God. Our goal should be to keep rejoicing, keep praising, and keep honoring God in all we do. Let's see how high God plans to take us.

**TIP**
Switch to soft plastics on your crappie jigs during the summer.

2 CHRONICLES 25:9

*The man of God answered, "The LORD is able*
*to give you much more than this."*

If you've ever been in any kind of competition in professional fishing, rodeo, racing, or any other pro sport, you've lost money by ounces or inches, or some little thing beyond your control. I've lost thousands and thousands of dollars over just an ounce or two over the years. We've all had situations in life where we've been stolen from, cheated, swindled, or just made dumb mistakes that really cost us.

I love today's scripture, and I've seen God perform it over and over in my life. Here, King Amaziah had hired a hundred thousand troops for one hundred talents of silver. (Almost four tons of silver!) The man of God told the king to send that army home, for the Lord was not with him. He was worried about the money but did follow God's advice. By the way, he won the battle. Always remember, the Lord is able.

**TIP**
Wheaties soaked in strawberry soda pop make excellent carp bait.

# JULY 9

EPHESIANS 4:26–27
*Do not . . . give place to the devil.*

**W**hen we have a sport like fishing in our lives, it is very rewarding. We develop friendships that last a lifetime. We spend quality time with our kids and, quite frequently, other family members as well. It's done outdoors, which is extremely good for us from a health standpoint. Just look at my buddies Roland Martin and Bill Dance, who fish almost every day past the age of eighty! As my buddy Richard Gene the Fishing Machine says, "Go fishing—it's good fer ya!"

Having fishing in our lives is rewarding. Having the devil in our lives is a disaster. He will use every trick, every attraction, every lie in his book to move in. Today's verse is dead in the middle of verses about ideas and actions we need to do or avoid (Ephesians 4:25–32). Read them and take them to heart. Don't let the devil into your life in any one of these situations!

**TIP**
Fish a swimming worm with heavy braid on grass flats.

DANIEL 1:8

*Daniel purposed in his heart that he would not defile himself with the portion of the king's delicacies, nor with the wine which he drank.*

To become better fishermen, we all have to put in some time on the water and some time studying how to become better. Most of us do this because of a deep passion for the game. We can't compromise. We need real dedication. We fight through bad weather, sore muscles, sunburned bodies, and bad results just to get better.

Daniel became super powerful, super wealthy, super famous, and honored. But as you can see from today's verse, he would not compromise along the way. We need to live our lives this way too. We may never actually be thrown to the lions, like Daniel was, but we will have plenty of chances to compromise Jesus. God sees us! Our future greatness and victory may depend on what we purpose in our hearts.

**TIP**
Add a larger hook to a jerkbait to allow it to sink deeper.

# JULY 11

1 PETER 5:8

*Be sober, be vigilant; because your adversary the devil walks about like a roaring lion, seeking whom he may devour.*

My friend Mike Frazier, who owns Camelot Bell Lake north of Waco, Texas, has another lake named Wolfpack. This lake was stocked with bass all weighing between ten and sixteen pounds. Both his lakes offer excellent opportunities to catch huge bass every day. In fishing, a wolfpack is a school of bass that roam a lake, shallow and deep, eating or devouring everything in sight.

In today's verse, Peter warned us the devil is that wolfpack and we are the shad, bluegill, crawfish, or whatever Satan is anxious to destroy. What is our protection? Well, one is to be on the lookout. Be vigilant. The devil may be hiding in something really attractive, ready to pounce. The other protection involves alcohol. We must stay sober to be safe from being gobbled up by the devil's tricks. Let's not become lunch for the devil.

**TIP**
Monofilament, not braid, is best on a bladed jig because of the stretch.

PROVERBS 18:12

*Before destruction the heart of a man is*
*haughty, and before honor is humility.*

One of the things I've noticed about the best fishermen is people will talk a lot about them. Not all is good. There is always some envy involved. But most of the talk is positive. This is true on the local level as well as at national bass-fishing events. Just the opposite is also true. Those not-so-good fishermen are always talking about themselves!

The Bible gives us a big warning about being haughty or prideful. As it says in today's verse, pride will destroy us. Pride is easy when we do well, and it feels good. We love it when folks brag about us, even if we are the ones doing the bragging. On the flip side, real humility from the heart will bring honor. Humility comes from winning and knowing and acknowledging exactly where that victory came from. Our victories are from God.

**TIP**

When fishing riprap, pay close attention to how far out the rocks extend under the water, and fish your lure all the way to where the rocks end.

1 CORINTHIANS 15:26–27

*The last enemy that will be destroyed is death. For*
*"He has put all things under His feet."*

Mayflies mostly hatch out in June or July, and some much later. A super place to fish is where mayflies are hatching. If you have kids, get them around a mayfly hatch for big-time bluegill fishing with an occasional bass or catfish thrown in. The problem (and benefit) is, mayflies don't live long. They are here, and, pretty quickly, they are gone.

Like mayflies, we are not here on earth for long. But in today's verse, Paul was saying God has put everything under Jesus' feet, including the last enemy to be destroyed: death. That was guaranteed when Jesus walked out of the grave. Think of it: death and the devil are under our feet too! We should live with total confidence and no fear. We will walk out of that grave as well. And we will spend forever with God.

**TIP**

Spotted bass often suspend in submerged treetops thirty to fifty feet deep in the summer.

2 CORINTHIANS 5:9

*We make it our aim, whether present or absent, to be well pleasing to Him.*

Summertime fishing can be really difficult—scorching hot days, little or no wind, and the fish seem to get harder to catch. We move to lighter lines and smaller plastics, and we fish mostly early and late in the day. Some move to night fishing. But through all this, we fish. We put in the work and effort to still catch them.

Pleasing God takes effort as well, and it should be a passion of every Christian to make it a priority. As today's verse says, this should be our goal every single day. Why would we want to do this? First, because of what God has done for us, creating us and sending Jesus to pay for our sins. Then, we're grateful for what God can and will do for us today, tomorrow, next week, next year, and for eternity. I can tell you, when we please God, God will please us!

> **TIP**
> Use a Ned rig in front of deep docks for summertime spotted bass.

## JULY 15

JEREMIAH 31:33
*"I will put My law in their minds, and write it on their hearts;
and I will be their God, and they shall be My people."*

My buddy Ricky Clunn, one of the greatest bass fishermen of all time, once told me he had so much information in his head about bass fishing that when he learned more, it crowded something out! I don't know about that, but I think as both of us get older, we just forget some of that stuff.

God says He has put His laws in our minds and on our hearts, whether we are saved or unsaved, walking with God or not, living in godly or ungodly ways. We absolutely know God's laws. We know how we should live. We know how we should treat others. We know we need a personal relationship with Jesus. Until Jesus comes back to earth, let's go out and live by what God has put in our minds and on our hearts.

> **TIP**
> Check under
> your trolling
> motor prop for
> fishing line.

1 TIMOTHY 5:25
*The good works of some are clearly evident, and*
*those that are otherwise cannot be hidden.*

It is amazing to me how quickly the word gets out when a hot new lure or technique hits the marketplace. How about when a hot new lake opens up in Florida, Mexico, or anywhere? I remember winning the 1986 B.A.S.S. Angler of the Year title mostly on a spinnerbait with two large willow leaf blades. It was astonishing how fast everyone started throwing those big willows. That secret didn't last long!

When we do something for someone or some cause, most folks notice. We like that. But what about the good we do in secret that nobody sees? Or if they do see, they might not care. Some will even criticize you for doing good. Paul was essentially telling Timothy in today's verse, "Don't worry about it. All the good you do will not be hidden." Hey, God sees. He knows. That is what is important.

> **TIP**
> Use your Power Poles to anchor and fish bare spots in grass flats.

# JULY 17

PROVERBS 17:22

*A merry heart does good, like medicine.*

It thrills me to see how much fun people have fishing. Once when I was fishing with Deion Sanders and Barry Switzer, Deion caught the first bass of the day, a four-pounder. He got as excited as if he had caught a twelve-pounder. My daughter, Sherri, when she was around thirteen, caught a seven-pound bass in Texas. She may have been happier than Deion!

We all know folks who just seem to be happy most all the time. Have you noticed that most of them are healthy as well? As you can see from today's proverb, God wants us to be happy and healthy. And He knows these two go hand in hand. We can have merry hearts, not just when good happens, like a big bass, but every day. We must take control of our hearts and minds and not let circumstances control us. Bad will happen. But we have the cure: our merry hearts.

**TIP**
Windblown, muddy water will generally slow down the bites.

PSALM 118:24

*This is the day the LORD has made; we will rejoice and be glad in it.*

Every fisherman can tell you about memorable days fishing. The day when we caught our largest fish, maybe a day when we caught the most. Many of mine are around bass tournaments, either my tournaments or Bass 'n Gal tournaments with Chris or Sherri. The greatest always had family involved. No matter what we are doing, some days are better than others.

What makes a day great? It's not the day at all. It's us and how each of us approaches that day. Today's psalm is a powerful verse to start every day with. We are alive in another day God created. We may be sick, broke, brokenhearted, angry, cheated, or lied to. But we are here, we have a God who loves us, and we have victory over death itself! It's our choice, so let's go out and make it a fabulous day.

**TIP**
White or chartreuse and white seem to be the best swim jig colors.

## JULY 19

ROMANS 8:37

*In all these things we are more than conquerors through Him who loved us.*

F lorida fishing was difficult for Chris and me in the early days of tournament fishing. The switch from man-made lakes with rivers, creeks, and dams was not easy. It was a real challenge to learn all the different types of grasses and how the bass related to them. The lack of much moving water and very small changes in the bottom contour were hard to get used to. Add to that, a Florida bass is different from the Texas (northern) largemouth with which we were familiar. But over time we conquered Florida fishing, and now we love it!

**TIP**

Using a clear plastic slip sinker ahead of a swimming worm is critical in heavy grass.

With God, there is nothing that can defeat us. Today's verse calls us "more than conquerors." If we belong to God, the devil can't defeat us. Health problems can't defeat us. Politics, enemies, even death can't defeat us. Let's live as champions today—because we are—and be all that God made us to be.

JAMES 5:16

*The effective, fervent prayer of a righteous man avails much.*

Over the years. I can't think of a single tournament day when I was too sick to fish, but I have missed practice days occasionally due to sickness. During the 1976 Angler of the Year battle, I was competing so hard that if I didn't have a pretty good string of fish going by 9:00 or 10:00 in the morning, I'd get physically sick and throw up! And then I'd keep on fishing.

In today's verse, James was speaking specifically about praying when we are sick or praying for someone who is sick. He was also singling out the prayers of the righteous. So we need to be right with God for our prayers to really be effective. But did you notice that these prayers become effective the moment we pray? Pray with passion, pray with righteousness, and your prayer will have supernatural power from the God who created us. Get ready—God is about to do something great.

**TIP**

A musky rod is best for punching heavy cover.

**PSALM 39:1**

*I will guard my ways, lest I sin with my tongue.*

At the 2019 FLW Tournament on Lakes Toho and Kissimmee, Chris and I had a fairly tough practice. Only one small area on Cypress Lake produced quite a few fish. If many found that area, it certainly wouldn't hold up for the full event. To my surprise, I was the only one fishing that area and won money on a combination of sinking worms, spinnerbaits, and flipping. I guarded that little area, and it really paid off.

There's another thing that must be guarded: our tongues. It's all but impossible to not sin with our tongues. This scripture tells us how to avoid it: guard our ways, our feelings, our anger, and how we act around those who are against us. When our feelings start taking over, we must zip it up and put a muzzle on our mouths. Remember, words are like bullets: once fired, we can't take them back! And they can be just as deadly. So let's guard our ways and tongues today.

**TIP**

Regular sonar shows more water area than chirp. It's best to use regular on your front fish finder.

JONAH 2:1

*Jonah prayed to the LORD his God from the fish's belly.*

As I have mentioned before, we fished the Sea of Galilee (Lake Gennesaret) in Israel. We went on invitation from the Israeli government to see if the freshwater fishing could be viable for tourists. We caught almost nothing, but it was a thrill to fish where Jesus walked on water, made coins appear in a fish's mouth, spoke fish into empty nets, preached, and fed thousands.

We also fished at Joppa, where Jonah started his famous journey. I wanted to catch that huge fish! Jonah was in that famous fish's belly for three days and nights before he prayed. I'm thinking Jonah might have been like us at times and only called on God as the last resort. Maybe we should call on God first today.

**TIP**
Cleaner, cooler water actually holds more oxygen.

2 CORINTHIANS 5:17

*If anyone is in Christ, he is a new creation;*
*old things have passed away.*

I got my hands on some hot new bait last year called the Mimic Impersonator. It's a clear plastic, lipless crankbait-type lure that has an insert to allow you to change the color of your bait without changing lures. One bait allows you a myriad of color selections. All my buddies had to have a Mimic and a few color inserts. As with most new products, we had some problems but worked them out, and now the bait works great.

When we are saved, we become new creations. This does not mean all things will be perfect and life will be a bowl of cherries. We will continue to sin, but now the Holy Spirit convicts us of sin, and we repent. We have a new Problem Solver who we can rely on every day.

**TIP**

Bass will follow the shad into flats in pockets (small coves) during late summer. Try a Mimic Impersonator there.

GENESIS 50:20

*You meant evil against me; but God meant it for good.*

It's a celebrated truth that fishermen don't always tell the truth. Some wonder if all fishermen lie, or all liars fish! Either way, in tournaments, it definitely happens. Some lie to protect what they know, and some to try to steer others in the wrong direction. The Bible tells us that even others' lies and actions against us can work for our good when God is on our side.

In Genesis we read that Joseph was thrown into a pit by his brothers, sold as a slave, accused of a crime, and put into prison. He was completely innocent. But the whole time, God was working on his behalf, and he became super successful. No matter your circumstances, never give up on God. It took years and years before Joseph reached what God had planned. Keep trusting. Keep believing. God is working on your victory right now—and it may be more than you can ever imagine.

## TIP

When fishing grass, peg your slip sinker with a bobber stop or toothpick.

JOHN 5:41

*"I do not receive honor from men."*

I can't begin to tell you how it feels to stand on the stage as the winner in a national bass tournament. Even more thrilling is to stand there as B.A.S.S. Angler of the Year after a long season of brutal competition. As amazing as that is (and God is the One who provides these victories), Jesus said that honor from men meant nothing to Him.

Jesus sought only to please God, and He lived His life to put a smile on His Father's face in everything He did. Those of us fortunate to have good relationships with our earthly fathers do the same thing. As kids, we looked to the stands when we got a hit or sunk a basket. We couldn't wait to show Dad a great report card. As adults, we still work at pleasing Dad even after he's gone on to heaven. Let's work hard today and every day to please our heavenly Father, just like Jesus did.

**TIP**

Around grass, listen for a popping sound, which indicates feeding bluegill. Obviously, use bluegill-colored lure!

DANIEL 3:18

*Let it be known to you, O king, that we do not serve
your gods, nor will we worship the gold image.*

Fishing is one of those sports that can create lots of passion. So much so that it can become one's golden image. To some, the passion can be hard to control. It can get in the way of family and friends. Passion for fishing has destroyed marriages and close family relationships. If you love fishing the way I love fishing, make sure you're keeping your priorities in order: faith, family, then fishing.

Our faith may never be tested like that of these three young Hebrew boys we read about in today's verse. They were about to be thrown into a burning furnace for refusing to worship a golden image. But then again, it may. Sometimes it seems our faith is tested on a daily basis. Can we develop these boys' faith in our God? You bet we can. And we should. We can see miracles happen just like this one.

**TIP**

Don't overlook topwater on calm, hot summer days, especially when clouds cover the sun.

JOB 19:20

*I have escaped by the skin of my teeth.*

Several times throughout my long life, I have escaped death on the water. Yes, several were by the skin of my teeth! When these accidents happen and we survive, we are very quick to thank God. Even non-Christians will do the same. And rightly so.

God does provide a hedge of protection around His children. He does provide legions of angels to help ward off danger around us. When Job uttered this now commonly used phrase in today's verse, he had lost his family, possessions, friends, and his health. His biggest concern was that God had forsaken him. We know the rest of the story. God had not left Job, and He restored to him everything he had lost. We need never have that forsaken feeling. God has promised to never leave or forsake us (Hebrews 13:5). If you belong to God, God will protect you—all the way through eternity.

**TIP**

On bluebird days, deep bass will hold close to deeper brush. Always try to fish over the top of them.

1 CORINTHIANS 3:16

*Do you not know that you are the temple of God
and that the Spirit of God dwells in you?*

Fifty-four years of tournament fishing forced me to stay in pretty good physical shape through the years. Mostly that involved running quite a bit, doing fifteen hundred stairs a day, and going on a no-carb/low-carb diet once every year or two. Although I still stay very active, I'm definitely not in shape to fish tournaments at the top level. It's possible to get there again, but it would take lots of work!

God wants us to be healthy. As you can see in today's verse, He lives in us, and that makes us holy. We are each a temple of God. He doesn't want us damaging that temple with alcohol, drugs, poor eating habits, or bad lifestyle choices. The next verse is scary: if we defile God's temple, God will destroy us! It seems to me we are actually destroying ourselves. Let's work today to not do that.

**TIP**

Use heavy hooks on jigs and worms when fishing heavy cover.

# JULY 29

ECCLESIASTES 2:26

*God gives wisdom and knowledge and joy to*
*a man who is good in His sight.*

During the twenty-one years of Bass 'n Gal national tournaments, I was amazed at how much knowledge and skill so many of the women developed over the years. You could just see them getting better. Their catches and their joy increased. We see the same thing with our kids and grandkids and great-grandkids.

We see in today's verse that all of this— wisdom, knowledge, and joy—is a gift from God. Here's the secret to these winning benefits: we need to be and do good in God's sight. Can we do that? You bet we can! We tell the truth. We're faithful. We're loving, forgiving, and humble. We help others. We are patient and kind. When we put a smile on God's heart, He will put a smile of wisdom, knowledge, and joy on ours. Let's do some good in God's sight today.

**TIP**

Find underwater shade to locate summertime bass—ledges, channels, submerged trees.

ISAIAH 37:36

*The angel of the LORD went out, and killed in the camp of
the Assyrians one hundred and eighty-five thousand.*

Spawning bluegill during the summer can be super
fun for even a seasoned bass pro, fast action for kids,
and a dream for most fly fishermen. The bluegill
is big and aggressive. But it's also a buffet
table for big bass. Find the bluegill spawning, and you find hungry bass.

Just as we find bass around spawning bluegill, we find angels around those
who trust God. Isaiah told us about King
Hezekiah, who trusted God, humbled
himself, and prayed. In today's verse God
responded and sent a powerful angel to wipe
out Hezekiah's enemy. That same God and
that same angel are available to us. Whatever
the enemy, whatever our problem, God has legions of
angels on call for our benefit. Our part is to be humble,
trust God, and pray. Get ready for angels to show up.

**TIP**
To improve
your skills
quicker, fish
lakes that have
lots of fish.

1 TIMOTHY 6:10

*The love of money is a root of all kinds of evil.*

My granddaughter Jordyn says that money can't buy happiness, but it sure can buy lots of fishing and hunting stuff that can make you happy! Chris has often said we have so much fishing tackle it's sinful. I am sure she is right. Thank goodness God forgives.

Having money and making money is not a sin. It is a gift from God. God creates wealth. It's the love of money that's the problem, as today's verse says. This chapter goes on to condemn greed, which will cause us sorrow and pain. The trick here is to make sure we are pursuing things of God and not money. When we actively pursue what God wants in our lives, He will reward us with wealth in many forms. It's easy to put money above God in our lives. One thing is certain: when we keep God first, He will always provide more than we need.

**TIP**

A blowhole in grass usually means a bass recently fed on a bluegill.

AUGUST

1 PETER 1:8–9

*You rejoice with joy . . . receiving the end of*
*your faith—the salvation of your souls.*

The rewards of fishing are many: health, happiness, family, friends, and for some, making a good living. God sure has blessed us in fishing. Yesterday, Chris said, "I'm going down to the dock to catch a few crappie. I have a headache. That should make it go away." I told her I'd go with her, since it didn't look like we would be doing anything else. What's amazing is, we caught forty-one, and her headache quit! Another godly reward.

Our simple, childlike faith in God has the greatest reward in the history of mankind: eternal salvation, living forever in the best place God ever created—heaven. If you've not accepted Jesus as your Lord and asked Him to save you, do that today. Your life will be changed and be better forever.

**TIP**

You can learn a lot by observing good tournament fishermen fish. Be sure to not get in their way.

MICAH 6:8

*What does the LORD require of you but to do justly, to
love mercy, and to walk humbly with your God?*

Summertime fishing usually requires fishing around,
under, and behind some boat docks. Cables, swim
ladders, and walkways enter the picture.
Light line and light action rods produce more bites, but how do you get
the bass or crappie out of this mess on skinny
line? Every situation is a little different, but
the trick is to let the fish swim away from
the dock on its own, even before you set the
hook if possible. Use the slightest amount of
pressure fighting the fish and most will swim
to open water. It's a pretty simple technique.

**TIP**
Always be
alert for
schooling
fish in late
summer.

Pleasing God is not that complicated. It
doesn't take skillful works or huge offerings, as you can
see from today's verse. Be honest in your relationships. Be
merciful to all you deal with. And stop patting yourself
on the back too much. Let's do our best to make God
happy today.

PROVERBS 31:28

*Her children rise up and call her blessed; her*
*husband also, and he praises her.*

My great-grandson Lightning loves to hunt and fish. He loves sports, especially football. But his thing is coming to the ranch to hunt and fish with Granddad. He's now a teenager and has a girlfriend. His mom, Jessica, told him that his girlfriend sure was pretty. Lightning said, "Yeah, but not as pretty as you, Mom!"

Proverbs 31 says an amazing wife is blessed by her children and that a virtuous wife is worth more than rubies. She has kindness on her tongue, she will be praised and honored, and her husband trusts her with his heart. Many have such a wife. I know I do! Many of you are that wife. I commend you. Guys, don't ever take them for granted. You old guys know that. You young guys, never let them go. Hold them tight. A godly woman is worth more than rubies, more valuable than a pot of gold.

**TIP**
Long, shallow bars on points are excellent but will produce even more in the summer.

REVELATION 19:11

*I saw heaven opened, and behold, a white horse. And*
*He who sat on him was called Faithful and True, and*
*in righteousness He judges and makes war.*

Almost every day in Florida during the summer, and fairly often all over the South, thunderstorms appear in the afternoon. The skies open and sudden downpours usually make fishing better and cool things down a bit. They're welcome occurrences. The risk is the dangerous lightning that comes with these storms.

**TIP**
Find concentrations of bluegill, and you've found bass as well!

The event in today's scripture won't be rain or lightning falling from heaven. It will be Jesus Himself returning. The sun will go dark, and the moon and stars will be gone. Christians will have already been raptured and, I believe, will witness this war between Jesus and Satan. Jesus will have come to judge a wicked world. Jesus will defeat the devil and throw him alive into the fiery pit. We'll have a ringside seat from heaven. Hallelujah!

1 KINGS 18:21

*How long will you falter between two opinions? If the*
*LORD is God, follow Him; but if Baal, follow him.*

You've heard me say that fishing is a thinking man's game. We make hundreds of decisions every day fishing. We decide based on factors that affect the fishing, like the type of water we are fishing, time of the year, what the water is doing, and the weather. The more we learn about these four things, the better decisions we'll make, and the more fish we will catch.

The words in today's verse were spoken by the prophet Elijah to the people of Israel, who teetered back and forth between worshiping God and the idol god Baal. And the people answered not a word; they failed to decisively choose God. Can we have Baals in our lives? You bet we can. Anything we place above God—money, careers, sports, fame, even fishing— becomes our Baal. If you have decided the Lord is your God, say so, and follow Him.

**TIP**
Some bass will move shallow only in the morning and evening.

### 1 SAMUEL 16:13

*Samuel took the horn of oil and anointed him in
the midst of his brothers; and the Spirit of the LORD
came upon David from that day forward.*

Looking back at some of the superstars of bass fishing,
I've found that each seems to get anointed by outdoor
writers and fellow competitors as being the very best
with certain baits. Roland Martin: plastic worm; Ricky Clunn: crankbait;
Tommy Biffle: jig; Ricky Green:
spinnerbait; Charlie Campbell: Zara
Spook. The truth is, each of these fishing
legends is an expert with all baits.

How would it be to be anointed by God
as the best? If you're a child of God, you are.
Today's verse tells how David was anointed
king as a teenager and given the Spirit of
God that day. He didn't become king until
years later. God has put His Spirit in you
and has victories for you. Those victories may be tomorrow or someday in the future. But they will come; God
has anointed you.

**TIP**
To find fish
shallow,
make sure
deep water
is close by.

# AUGUST 7

GALATIANS 2:20

*I have been crucified with Christ; it is no longer
I who live, but Christ lives in me.*

Our job in fishing is to simulate a live baitfish with
an artificial lure. How do we do that? Cadence and
rhythm. Mother Nature has things balanced. Baitfish
move in a certain rhythm and
cadence. Duplicate that, and
you've brought a dead plastic bait
to life. That pop, pop-pop, pop, pop-pop
cadence or rhythmic swish, swish, swish,
swish is magic. Master cadence and rhythm,
and it's game on.

Like bringing life to that artificial bait,
we have crucified our old sinful selves and
been filled with the life and righteousness of
Jesus Christ Himself. As today's verse says,
Christ lives in us. We have been resurrected
to perfection with Him. We are empowered
by Jesus in us and enjoy that same victory over sin and
death. Christ in me—perfect!

**TIP**

Shallow-water
fish are less
affected by
current than
deeper-water
ledge fish.

HEBREWS 2:18

*In that He Himself has suffered, being tempted,*
*He is able to aid those who are tempted.*

Sometimes, you just have to make a bass bite. Take dominion over the fish and will it into striking. How can you do that? Some magical supernatural power? I wish! I've found multiple casts into really good spots can often make them bite. Don't multiple cast every spot, only the very best-looking ones. Temptation will finally be too much for that fish.

Temptation is a tough one, and it can cause us to get hooked into some pretty terrible things—some that can cost us our families, friends, jobs, even our lives. How can we fight these temptations? The same way Jesus did: taking His Father's advice. In today's verse God said He will help. He gave us His Holy Spirit for these times. When you hear that small voice inside saying, *Don't lie; don't cheat; don't compromise; don't say it,* listen; it's God Himself trying to help.

**TIP**
Use Google Earth to study a new lake before you fish.

PHILIPPIANS 3:20
*Our citizenship is in heaven, from which we also
eagerly wait for the Savior, the Lord Jesus Christ.*

I've been blessed to fish many different waters all over
the world. I've fished the waters Jesus walked on in
Israel, and I've also fished in Africa, Colombia, Cuba,
Venezuela, Canada, Guatemala, Mexico, the Virgin
Islands, and the list goes on. We
truly have the very best fishing in
the world right here in America,
from sea to shining sea. It's heaven on
earth to people who love to fish.

No matter how long we live here
on earth, it's a short time compared to
eternity. Today's scripture reminds us
that we are citizens of heaven. But while
we are here, we realize Jesus could come
back any second. We need to live our lives
as if that day is today. Will Jesus find us
honoring Him in all we are doing? That's
going to be one glorious flight to heaven!

**TIP**
Pay close
attention to
changes in water
color. This can
be a clue to
what color lure
to use and even
where to fish.

PSALM 27:14

*Wait on the Lord; be of good courage, and*
*He shall strengthen your heart.*

It's an incredible feeling to be involved as one of the last few competitors weighing in on the final day of a national tournament. If you're in that group, you have a chance to win. If you are last to weigh in, your odds are great. But the wait will make your knees shake!

As we began the journey after my beautiful wife, Chris, had her stroke, this was one of God's verses that sustained me. It's hard for anyone to be really strong when your world is turned upside down. We want normal, and we want it quickly! We want strength to make it through each moment. I learned to be patient, to wait on God. He has more than Superman strength. God has supernatural strength. Whatever struggle you are in, however weak and hurting your heart may be, wait on the Lord. Help is on the way. Heavenly help!

**TIP**
The tougher the fishing, the slower we need to fish.

## AUGUST 11

ROMANS 12:21

*Do not be overcome by evil, but overcome evil with good.*

The dog days of summer can make for some really hard fishing. When the temperatures start hovering around the hundred-degree mark every day, an added problem is dead calm. If you can't go several hundred miles north, you might want to look around for a river to fish. The moving water provides some cool, and with rivers being narrow, shade is often available, helping you overcome the heat.

Today's scripture talks about how to overcome the heat of evil. How do we pay back those who have done us wrong? We don't pay them back. We leave that to God. What we do is overcome. And we do that with the Spirit God gives us when we are saved. When we are lied to, cheated, stolen from, talked down to, or disrespected, we do just the opposite. Now we're talking! Now we're walking the walk that Jesus walked and gave to us. Praise God: *Thank You, Lord.*

TIP

Overcome bad practice days in tournaments by going to all new water.

LUKE 6:31

*"Just as you want men to do to you, you also do to them likewise."*

I f you night fish, as many do during the summer, you will notice the bite is usually best right at dark and then slows down. It does take a bit for the fish's eyes to adjust to the dark. A good bet is to fish that last hour or so before dark; it can be the formula for success.

Today's verse is perhaps the best formula for success in the Bible if you want to become the person God wants you to be. That's my goal in this life. It will also make you a better friend, spouse, parent, boss, or employee—whatever you are trying to succeed in. The golden rule is to do to others as you would have them do to you. Let me add this: speak to and talk about others as you want them to speak to and talk about you. That's my goal for today.

**TIP**
To fish deeper quicker, use a single Colorado blade.

GALATIANS 2:6

*God shows personal favoritism to no man.*

As I've mentioned, a spinnerbait is my favorite bait. There have been tournaments where I've never made a cast with any other lure. There have been years when I've caught 60 to 70 percent of all my fish on that magic bladed bait. Those tournaments and those years were some of my best for cashing checks. I definitely have had a love affair with a spinnerbait!

Does God have a favorite person? You bet He does. It's you . . . and me. I believe God loves each of us to the max, more than we could ever imagine. He calls Himself our Father. And just like any father, He wants the very best for us. He's working today to handle every problem we have, to heal every relationship, and to make our lives better. Live life today as if you are God's favorite child and most important person. Because you are. We all are!

**TIP**

Swimbaits and flukes weighted with a nail weight are dynamite around docks.

PSALM 141:3

*Set a guard, O LORD, over my mouth; keep*
*watch over the door of my lips.*

We use weedguards on jigs to keep from snagging or hanging up in heavy cover. We cut the front treble off square-bills as a way to get through heavy brush. Plus, although it dampens vibration, spinnerbait wires have become longer to guard against hang-ups.

Wouldn't it be fabulous if we had a simple lip guard of some sort to guard over words we speak? How would it be if we spoke no hurtful words, no discouraging words, no prideful words, no angry words? Today's verse tells me we can, but we need God's help, and we get it simply by asking. Let's make it a part of our prayers to ask God for that help every day. I'm believing that will keep us free from lots of snags and hang-ups we face in everyday life.

**TIP**

The new telescopic long poles make crappie and bluegill fishing even more fun!

PSALM 27:13

*I would have lost heart, unless I had believed that I would see the goodness of the LORD in the land of the living.*

To catch really big fish, giant bass, we use LiveScope technology on our fish finders. We are not trying to catch lots of fish, but we are searching for the biggest bass in the lake. Sure, we need patience; but more important, we must know it will work. We've made it happen before. Keep looking. Keep believing.

David, in today's verse, said his confidence in God was coming directly from what he believed. He was sure he would see God's goodness. When we believe, we too, as Christians, will see God's goodness. Sure, we are saved for eternity; but God wants to pour His goodness on us now—goodness in all aspects of our lives: our health, our families, relationships, finances, all of it. Our part is simply to believe. Claim God's goodness today by believing.

**TIP**

Some fish will always stay shallow in lakes with regular current.

PSALM 84:11

*The LORD God is a sun and shield; the LORD will give grace and glory; no good thing will He withhold from those who walk uprightly.*

The good thing about fishing is it brings families and friends together. Another good thing about fishing is it brings us closer to God and His creation. Yet another good thing about fishing is the competition, both friendly and professional. And even more good things about fishing are the peace and tranquility we get. I could go on and on.

In today's verse, God promised to withhold no good thing from us if we will do just one thing: walk uprightly. This can actually be done, and it should be our goal every day. When we do, we will see God's favor, God's help, God's blessings raining down on us as never before. Let's walk uprightly today and see what good God has planned.

**TIP**
You can see yellow braid better for those strikes you don't feel. Be sure to use a leader.

NEHEMIAH 5:19

*Remember me, my God, for good, according to*
*all that I have done for this people.*

I remember a B.A.S.S. tournament back in 1986 on the Saint Lawrence River and Lake Ontario in upstate New York. As luck would have it, a hurricane came through the second day and turned Lake Ontario into a deadly ocean. I knocked my Mercury's lower unit off twenty miles away from weigh-in. Jim Golden, from Golden's Marina, launched a boat, rescued us, and took us to the weigh-in! Because of the good he did for me, I was able to get there in time and won the tournament.

**TIP**
Use a swim jig in shallow willow grass.

In today's verse Nehemiah was boldly asking God to do good for him because of what he had done for God's people. God has given each of us that right through Jesus to ask God boldly for good according to the good we have done for others.

1 KINGS 17:14

*"The bin of flour shall not be used up, nor shall the jar of oil run dry, until the day the LORD sends rain on the earth."*

My daughter, Sherri, and I were fly rod fishing the Frazier River one fall. Way up the river we found a secluded hole loaded with sockeye salmon. We caught fish after fish, but the hole never ran dry. In fact, just the opposite: more salmon showed up, almost by the minute. There were more fish in that hole when we quit than when we started.

**TIP**

Fish docks with lights at night.

In today's verse Elijah had asked a lady to prepare him a meal with what little flour and oil she had left during a great famine. But he promised a blessing if she would only trust God and believe. She did, and a miracle happened every day until God sent rain: the flour and oil never ran out. What miracle is God waiting to do in our lives if we just believe and trust Him?

## AUGUST 19

JOHN 14:16

*"I will pray the Father, and He will give you another*
*Helper, that He may abide with you forever."*

How about if you could take a top-of-the-line pro bass fisherman with you on every fishing trip? Folks like Roland Martin, Bill Dance, Hank Parker, or Kevin VanDam? Would you catch more fish? Of course you would. What if you had access to all of them and everything they know? Wow. That would be even better. I'd sure sign up for that!

What if you could have God with you every second of every minute of every hour of all your days? Well, that's exactly what you get when you get saved: a helper, God's Holy Spirit with God's infinite wisdom and knowledge to guide you through life day by day, 24–7. Every decision, every thought, every word from your mouth can be guided by God Himself. But just like fishing with the pros, you've got to listen and take God's advice.

**TIP**
Grass canopies block sunlight, which causes bass to congregate in the thin grass below.

1 CORINTHIANS 6:11

*You were washed, . . . you were sanctified, . . . you were justified*
*in the name of the Lord Jesus and by the Spirit of our God.*

So many of my fishing friends caught the coronavirus: Jimmy Sites, Roland Martin, David Dudley, and many more. Also, a number of friends on our social media platforms caught it. Many used their blood with its antibodies to help cure others. People's lives were saved, washed by the blood of someone who had suffered through the virus, but the donor didn't need to die to help.

It's amazing to think about this parallel of Jesus using His precious blood to save a dying world. Here, two thousand years later, that blood is still saving lives. Maybe God is reminding us what power is in the blood of Jesus. It's power that will sanctify us and cleanse every sin we commit, past, present, and future. There's great victory over sin and death in every single drop of the blood of Jesus.

**TIP**
Use red or black blades when night fishing.

MARK 9:23

*Jesus said to him, "If you can believe, all things*
*are possible to him who believes."*

Isn't it exciting when we first get our hands on a hot
new bait that we hear is fantastic? How about a new
technique that you've just learned? Or the incredible electronics that seem to get better each year? We're excited.
We believe this new bait, technique, or equipment will
instantly help us catch more fish. Of
course, that excitement often fades if
we don't whack 'em like we thought we
would.

How about our belief in the God
who saved us? Can that belief, real belief,
fade over time? The father of the demon-
possessed boy who was asking Jesus for
help said, "Lord, I believe; help my unbelief" (Mark 9:24). And he had just seen
a miracle! Think about why you believe
and who you believe, and get ready for
miracles. As today's verse says, all things
are possible.

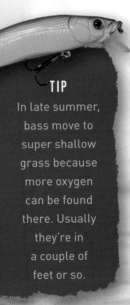

**TIP**

In late summer,
bass move to
super shallow
grass because
more oxygen
can be found
there. Usually
they're in
a couple of
feet or so.

MATTHEW 20:32

*Jesus stood still and called them, and said,*
*"What do you want Me to do for you?"*

We get lots of inquiries from companies about helping them with a product or line of products. Most are from small companies trying to get started, but some are from companies needing a bigger share of the market-place. This is because of our long-lasting presence on national television, and due even more to our rapidly growing social media channels. Some we can help; others we can't. But we can't help any of them immediately.

**TIP**
Points near bends in rivers or creeks hold bass all summer long.

In response to Jesus' question in today's verse, "What do you want Me to do for you?" the blind men said, "Lord, that our eyes may be opened" (Matthew 20:33). Miraculously, Jesus opened their eyes, and they could see immediately. Jesus did not need to make a post, do a video, or produce a commercial! This is the God we serve, and Jesus is asking us that same question. What do we want Him to do?

## AUGUST 23

GENESIS 26:12

*Isaac sowed in that land, and reaped in the same year a hundredfold; and the LORD blessed him.*

One of the interesting things about this sport is the way fish reproduce. Fish reproduce more fish by the thousands. God made it this way so we would have fish for food. With programs like catch-and-release for bass, size and quantity limits, and superior water conservation here in America, our waters are teeming with fish.

God showed us in today's verse, early on in the Bible, what happens when we sow the seeds of God. He will bless. When we sow kindness, He will multiply that. When we sow love, He multiplies that. When we spread joy, peace, and happiness, God blesses it. God multiplies. When we sow offerings and tithes, God blesses. God multiplies. Whatever your heart desires, sow that seed today and watch God bless it a hundredfold this very year.

**TIP**

When fishing ledges with current, position your boat downstream and cast upstream from the fish.

JIMMY HOUSTON

ISAIAH 41:13

*"I, the LORD your God, will hold your right hand,*
*saying to you, 'Fear not, I will help you.'"*

I took my longtime friend Gus Rhoton fishing when he was ninety-six. The lake and the walkway were flooded. We had to walk a long two-by-twelve board to get on the walkway to the dock where the boat was. Gus absolutely would not walk that plank. Finally, his son Jerry and I agreed to wade in the water and hold his hands on each side. He agreed, he successfully walked across, and we caught more than forty bass that day.

> **TIP**
> Popping topwater baits work excellent on summer flats.

Did you know that God will always hold your hand? In today's scripture He said, "Fear not." Fear is a mighty weapon of political parties, the government, friends, enemies, even husbands and wives. Fear is a tool of the devil. He puts it in the hands and hearts of others to kill and destroy us. But our weapon is bigger and more powerful. His name is Jesus.

# AUGUST 25

## JOHN 15:15

*"No longer do I call you servants, for a servant does not know what his master is doing; but I have called you friends, for all things that I heard from My Father I have made known to you."*

Friends are like that old American Express commercial—priceless! The 2020 pandemic caused lots of good in fishing. More folks were fishing than ever before, many with close friends. It's pretty easy to social distance in a Tracker or Ranger bass boat! But many friends quit fishing together. Many quit doing anything together, with no face-to-face talks.

What would it be like to talk to Jesus face-to-face? We will look into the eyes of Jesus one day, but not now. But we can speak to God as a friend, and we should when we pray. We should speak to Jesus as a friend. He said, "I have called you friends." And He will talk back as a friend. Not out loud, but inside your heart. He's given us His Holy Spirit and placed Him inside us to visit as a friend. What a friend we have in Jesus!

**TIP**

Fish steeper banks as the lake level drops.

LUKE 8:39

*"Return to your own house, and tell what*
*great things God has done for you."*

Family is the glue that holds the American cul-
ture together as we know it. It's definitely
the key to any outdoorsy household as we
spend hours, days, and years teaching our
kids and grandkids how to fish and hunt.

The story today's verse comes from is
one of my favorites in the Bible. As Jesus and
His disciples were about to step ashore from
a boat, a naked, dirty, crazy man possessed
by demons came running down the mountain. They all shrank back, except Jesus, who
calmly walked up to him, visited with him,
and cast out the legion of demons. Later,
sitting around a fire, dressed and completely
healed, this man asked to join Jesus' ministry and to follow Him. As powerful as the man's testimony was, Jesus
sent him home to tell his own family about Jesus. We
teach our kids and grandkids about fishing. Make sure
you are teaching yours about Jesus even more.

**TIP**
Look for
crawfish
holes on
clay banks.

# AUGUST 27

## PSALM 46:1
*God is our refuge and strength, a very present help in trouble.*

We all have certain go-to baits and tactics when things don't go just right on the water. I actually have several, and how I use them depends on whether I'm just fun fishing, tournament fishing, or making a television show. It might be a small jig and worm, a spinnerbait, point hopping, or I might even change lakes. Some anglers just quit when things go wrong. Don't quit! Today's little verse sums up a lot to me. When things don't go right in life, we need a place of safety, a refuge. That's God and His Word. And while we're there in God's Word, those words will encourage and make us stronger as that trouble becomes weaker and less of a problem. But here's the biggie: God is at work helping us solve the problem. He's doing things and setting up situations that we never dreamed of. And at just the right time, our trouble is gone.

**TIP**
In grass, it's better to fish frogs really, really slow.

JOHN 13:35

*"By this all will know that you are My disciples,*
*if you have love for one another."*

I've talked often about how awesome a lifelong fishing partner I have in my wife, Chris. She's not only a world champion bass angler herself who knows how to locate and catch fish; she's just a lot of fun to fish with. And she doesn't get hung up very often! What a blessing. People don't have to be around us too much to see how much we love each other.

People shouldn't have to be around us much to tell how much we love God and that we count ourselves among Jesus' disciples. As Jesus says in today's verse, we show it by our love for one another. We smile at everyone we meet, say a prayer for the hurting, share a kind word, an encouraging word, an uplifting word to those who are down. We lend a helping hand when needed, and we demonstrate sincere concern and sharing to those who need Jesus.

**TIP**
Fish a spinnerbait fast at night on flats.

JONAH 1:3

*Jonah arose to flee to Tarshish from the presence of the LORD.*

B ass fishing requires some stealth, especially when the water is clear and the fish are shallow. Particularly you need stealth when the bass are spawning and are near or on the beds. Often, if they see or feel the presence of a boat, they're out of there!

Everyone knows the story about Jonah. God told him to go preach to the folks at the evil city Nineveh, where God had prepared an amazing revival. It was any preacher's dream trip. God might just save all the people there in Nineveh. (He actually did.) But it wasn't for Jonah. He split and ran from God, and it nearly cost him his life. God is always talking to each of us Christians also. Are we listening? Are we obeying? Do we run when God tells us to speak to someone? To encourage someone? Maybe to pray for them or pray with them? Why not take a minute next time you feel like running, and obey instead?

**TIP**

After that productive early-morning bite is over, don't be afraid to fish deeper.

PROVERBS 27:10

*Do not forsake your own friend or your father's friend.*

My dad was a lifelong versatile fisherman. His first love was crappie fishing, but bass ran a close second. And he could really catch bass. He hosted the 1962 World Series of Sport Fishing at our resort on Tenkiller Lake. Virgil Ward won that championship and started his popular *Championship Fishing* show on television. So Dad was thrilled when I started winning bass tournaments.

Dad died in January 1990. A patriarch of the entire lake area, he had tons of friends. But he had a few special friends he had fished with often, and many more he had guided fishing for years.

God pops today's proverb into my head often, and I make it a point to visit with Dad's closest friends and even with some of Dad's old guide customers at tackle shows. If a friend of your father comes to mind today, you might want to pay him a visit. It could be God asking you.

**TIP**
Search out smaller underwater structures with your locator.

## 2 TIMOTHY 3:16

*All Scripture is given by inspiration of God, and is profitable for doctrine, for reproof, for correction, for instruction in righteousness.*

Some of us have hundreds of fishing lures. Can we actually catch a fish on all of them? You bet we can. The trick is using the right lure under the right conditions at the right time. We don't have to be using the best lure we have in every situation, but every lure we have will catch fish.

Paul was telling us in today's scripture that all of God's Word is for good—every single word. The word in this verse that I like is *profitable*. That means God's Word will make us better off. Not financially, although He will provide; but it will make us better off as people, as spouses, as parents. God created us to be exceptional people, full of joy and happiness. Whenever you feel down or have a problem, grab that Bible and open it anywhere. God will do the rest.

**TIP**
It's courteous to not throw at a fish your partner misses.

SEPTEMBER

# SEPTEMBER 1

ISAIAH 54:17

*No weapon formed against you shall prosper.*

One of the benefits of fishing a lot is that you just become better at it. There's not much that will stop you from catching fish. Different types of lures, water conditions, bad weather—you've seen all these and learned how to handle them. You have the tools and knowledge for success.

God has given His people all the tools we need to succeed against whatever this life, our enemies, or even the devil comes against us with. When folks say bad things about us, God will turn them around for our good. When people cheat or steal from us, God will pay us back double. When we have health problems, God is the great Healer. I've been fired from jobs, and God has always given me something better. We fight our battles with a shield of faith and the sword of God's Holy Spirit. No weapon can match that power.

LUKE 10:37

*And he said, "He who showed mercy on him." Then*
*Jesus said to him, "Go and do likewise."*

Chris and I once had a generator quit on our old truck after midnight near Poteau, Oklahoma. No generator, no headlights. I walked to town and found a closed auto parts store. We had no cell phones, but somehow I located the owner by pay phone. He got out of bed, came to the store, and sold me a generator. Even drove me back to my truck and helped me install it. Now, that's mercy.

Today's scripture contains the last two statements in a conversation between Jesus and a lawyer who was asking questions to trick Jesus. The lawyer asked Jesus about obtaining eternal life, quoted scripture correctly about loving your neighbor as yourself, and then asked, "Who is my neighbor?" (Luke 10:29). Jesus answered with the story of the good Samaritan. Jesus is telling us today to show mercy. Let's be that good Samaritan!

**TIP**
Learn to cast under docks for hard-to-get fish, both bass and crappie.

## SEPTEMBER 3

JOHN 15:11

*"These things I have spoken to you, that My joy may*
*remain in you, and that your joy may be full."*

If there is anything more joy filled than fishing, it might be kids swimming in the lake. I remember one practice day on Lake Guntersville in Alabama. Chris and I got tickled watching kids jump off the top of a big dock in Browns Creek. They were screaming and laughing, having a blast. Obviously, they were also scaring all the fish away, but we loved it. One girl would run right to the edge and stop. She never did make that jump, and nobody pushed her!

I believe that God gets tickled watching you when you're full of joy. Jesus spent years giving His advice and wisdom to His closest friends so they could be full of joy. That's His purpose for you and me. It says so right in today's verse. That's how important our happiness is to God. Let's share that happiness and joy today.

> **TIP**
> Scroll speed on locators needs to be set relatively fast.

1 CORINTHIANS 15:57

*Thanks be to God, who gives us the victory through our Lord Jesus Christ.*

My wife, Chris, has won lots of Bass 'n Gal Tournaments, seven Bass 'n Gal Angler of the Year titles, three or four Classics, and twenty to twenty-five boats. We never counted them! She was the first woman ever elected to the Bass Fishing Hall of Fame! I never saw her stand onstage and accept these winning trophies without thanking God. She often talked about fish falling out of heaven. She knew where the victories came from.

Today's scripture is not talking about winning money, trophies, boats, or accolades. God was speaking here about victory over death. Did you know this life on earth is only temporary? Did you know you and I will live forever in either heaven or hell? I believe when we last close our eyes here, we open them looking into the eyes of Jesus or the eyes of the devil. Our choice. Make Jesus your Lord and Savior today.

**TIP**

Use larger swimbaits on deeper brush piles, 10–12 feet and deeper.

# SEPTEMBER 5

2 SAMUEL 22:33

*God is my strength and power, and He makes my way perfect.*

Today's young fishermen are fantastic. They start tournament competitions in high school and just get better and better. Are they as good or better than those earlier superstars? How about Hank Parker, Ricky Green, Bill Dance, Roland Martin, Denny Brauer, Ricky Clunn, Kevin VanDam? The list could fill pages. I don't know, but I do know one thing young and old have in common: none are perfect.

**TIP**
Bluegill often spawn on the shallow ends of islands.

I love today's verse. It doesn't say God makes me perfect, although He will one glorious day in heaven. He makes my way perfect, this path through life I'm traveling. God's strength and power are available to you and me. He is keeping me safe in an evil world, putting me with the right people at the right times, healing me when I'm sick, directing my decisions, and much, much more. God is working to make your way and mine perfect. Right now.

JIMMY HOUSTON

JAMES 3:17

*The wisdom that is from above is first pure, then peaceable, gentle, willing to yield, full of mercy and good fruits, without partiality and without hypocrisy.*

Flying over lakes in a single-engine airplane used to be an extremely popular way to learn about lakes. It was legal and still is in some situations. Now we have drones, and most are not allowed in tournaments. Pretty much everyone uses Google Earth to see water from up high. What if we could get lake and fishing information from God Himself? Well, He might just do that occasionally, but mostly that won't happen.

But we can get something better— wisdom from God. He gives wisdom that is first and foremost pure. I've got to tell you: if you're younger, some of the other characteristics listed in today's verse will seem almost impossible for you, especially that "willing to yield" one. Honestly, all are impossible without God in your heart, soul, and mind. Let's all work on perfecting this wisdom from above.

> **TIP**
> Take a boat ride around the areas you plan to fish, checking water temperatures.

# SEPTEMBER 7

EZEKIEL 37:13

*"You shall know that I am the LORD, when I have opened your graves, O My people, and brought you up from your graves."*

**B**ack in the early days of B.A.S.S., in 1969, I believe, Rip Nunnery and Gerald Blanchard brought in two amazing limits of bass from Lake Eufaula, Alabama. One boat, if I remember right, had 184 pounds of large-mouth bass! We had a fifteen-bass limit then, so that many pounds was unimaginable. They were fishing an old, submerged graveyard. Empty graves, shrubs, trees, and fences were all loaded with huge bass.

**TIP**

When bass hang up in grass, go get them!

Today's scripture about graves was written around 580 BC. Ezekiel was in a valley full of dry bones. God had Ezekiel speak to these bones, and they joined together miraculously and came to life to form a great army! One breath of God breathed life into thousands. One breath of God's favor can change your life and mine. Keep God first, and you can't imagine what He might do next.

ROMANS 12:11

*. . . not lagging in diligence, fervent in spirit, serving the Lord.*

When we are doing something we love, like fishing, we go at it full-bore—hook, line, and sinker! We fish hard and with great fervor. We take the bad days in stride and can't wait to go again. We do this because we love fishing.

God wants us to serve Him with that same kind of passion, that same fervor and enthusiasm. He wants us to be diligent. I take that to mean that every day we should serve God with this enthusiasm. I believe God wants us to carry that into everything we do. Carry that sparkle, that love, that enthusiasm into your job, your marriage, and all your relationships and watch God change your life for the better. Watch Him work as your coworkers become nicer and friendlier, your family seems to have more fun, and more folks enjoy being around you! God will start rewarding you in ways you never imagined.

**TIP**
Fish are always moving in tidal waters.

## SEPTEMBER 9

JOHN 6:9

*There is a lad here who has five barley loaves and two*
*small fish, but what are they among so many?*

Since the advent of the Garmin LiveScope, fishermen
have begun targeting larger fish. It turns out that
larger bass usually are alone, quite often suspended above
brush or logs. They are mostly
above schools of shad in the colder
months and not below them. They
spook easily and often run from our baits.

Today's scripture is about Jesus performing the miracle of feeding over five
thousand men with one boy's lunch. It is
interesting that the fish weren't big like
the ones we scope out nowadays: they were
most likely tilapia, under a pound. Also, it
appears the boy gave Jesus the fish without
any argument. This could be the childlike
faith it takes to come to Jesus. I like to think he caught
those fish himself. This young fisherman didn't just share
his catch; he gave it all, plus his bread! Give Jesus your all
today, and get ready for a miracle.

**TIP**

Search for
murky or
muddy water
that is clearing.

ACTS 3:19

*Repent therefore and be converted, that your sins may be blotted out,*
*so that times of refreshing may come from the presence of the Lord.*

It is good to keep an eye out for birds when fishing. Blue herons are always a giveaway for baitfish in shallow water. Definitely fish a bank that has multiple blue herons. They fish for a living. Seagulls circling and diving in the water indicate baitfish being pushed to the surface by bigger fish. Loons and cormorants on the water and diving under are feeding on fish. Even blackbirds will give away last night's mayfly hatch. Find the birds, catch fish. Birds are present around bait.

God wants to be present in us. The moment we are saved, our sins are erased, and God's Holy Spirit comes to live in us. God's Spirit guides us to refreshing times of success and victory. His presence leads us into becoming better people who make smarter decisions and live abundantly.

**TIP**
Bass often move to deeper water when the shad spawn ends.

# SEPTEMBER 11

## 2 CHRONICLES 20:15

*Do not be afraid nor dismayed because of this great multitude, for the battle is not yours, but God's.*

As the water cools, bass tend to bunch up in deeper water. On most lakes, drop shot rigs work great. Use light line and a small sinker on the bottom with a worm hook twelve to twenty inches above that weight. Small worms, nose hooked, should fool big numbers of fish, and the bass battle will soon be on.

**TIP**
Fish isolated grass patches near deep water with a black frog on cloudy days.

Life is full of battles. People say bad things about us, or we might have family issues or job problems. King Jehoshaphat faced sure defeat in battle. After hearing the words from today's verse from God, reminding them that the battle was His, all the people believed and worshiped. The next day, God completely destroyed the army without the people even having to fight. We serve that same God. Whatever your battle, it is God's battle—you don't have to fight it.

JIMMY HOUSTON

JOB 26:10

*He drew a circular horizon on the face of the waters,*
*at the boundary of light and darkness.*

Here's a secret not many people know: if we will concentrate our fishing where two things in the water come together, we will catch more fish. It could be a rocky bank meeting a smooth bank, a grass line ending, corners of boat docks, or junction-type areas. Even dingy or muddy water meeting clear water.

**TIP**
For bigger fish in heavy cover, try flippin' that cover.

Job spoke the words in today's verse hundreds of years before humans learned the earth was round. They believed it was flat. Yet Job described a circular earth with sunrise and sunset. God had given this amazing insight to a blameless and righteous man. How incredible is that? Can God still give that kind of insight to righteous folks today? I believe He can and does. We just need to get right with Him and invite God into all of our lives, not just parts of them. He might just let us in on some secrets.

# SEPTEMBER 13

## 1 CORINTHIANS 1:18

*The message of the cross is foolishness to those who are perishing;*
*but to us who are being saved it is the power of God.*

Hooksetting is an integral part of bass fishing. You don't need to be big, strong, and powerful to create effective hooksets. The key is not brawn; it is speed. The more rod speed you develop, the better your hookset. Some baits require almost no hookset, like the sweeping action of a Carolina rig. Although we are setting a super-sharp hook into the fish, it feels no pain; fish are cold-blooded.

Totally opposite was the crucifixion of the Son of God. Being crucified was the most demeaning, most painful way the Romans knew how to kill a man. Yet that cross where Jesus died has become the most powerful symbol of Christianity. I wear one around my neck. It shows us the ever-present power of God over death. Jesus overcame death on that cross by His Father's power. We who are saved will do the same.

> **TIP**
> Use tenth-ounce jig heads and small worms in shallow water.

2 TIMOTHY 3:3
*. . . unloving, unforgiving, slanderers, without self-*
*control, brutal, despisers of good . . .*

**W**ow! Today's verse surely doesn't sound like Paul was talking about a fisherman. How about a group of fifteen or twenty fishermen? Could we find one or more of those traits in some of them? Put all of these sins in one person and we may be talking about the devil himself. Paul warned that in the end times, this is what men will become.

The surrounding verses add more characteristics, speaking of people who are lovers of money, boastful, lovers of themselves, haughty, unholy, traitors, and lovers of pleasure rather than God. How many of those will we find in our small group of fishermen? More important, how many of these things are we guilty of at times? When all these things manifest in mankind at large, the end is close; Jesus is coming back. We can't change the world, but we can watch closely and guard against any of these evil characteristics getting inside us.

**TIP**
Power Pole down to fish isolated holes in patches of lily pads.

# SEPTEMBER 15

PROVERBS 12:14

*A man will be satisfied with good by the fruit of his mouth.*

At an FLW tournament on Lake Kissimmee in Florida, most competitors were locking through to the lower lakes. Only about a dozen boats locked through at a time. With 180 boats, it was a train wreck ready to happen. I was about boat fifteen to the lock and almost made that first lock through but was at the front for the second until other competitors arrived. There was lots of pushing and shoving. My boat was pushed to the side.

I said not a cross word, was nice to everyone, but locked through in the last lock almost two hours later!

Life pushes us aside just about every day; I've seen this same scenario play out with shopping carts. How we react with our words is critical. Will we speak words of love, peace, joy, and encouragement? Or will we speak the opposite? By the way, I caught a huge limit of bass that day. Highly satisfying.

**TIP**
Throw darker colors on cloudy days.

MATTHEW 25:34

*"Come, you blessed of my Father; inherit the kingdom prepared for you from the foundation of the world."*

A killer bait that works from shallow down to very deep water is a Scrounger Head Jig. This jig, made by Luck-E-Strike, is a wobble head–type jig that adds action to any soft plastic attached. Most popular is a swimbait. The secret is that it is always wobbling and vibrating, and it puts dynamite action on the soft plastic. The most used technique is to let it fall to the bottom and slow wind it back in. It's one of the easier baits to fish.

It is even easier to inherit the kingdom of God. He created heaven just for us. It is simpler than fishing a Scrounger too. We simply acknowledge Jesus as God's Son, repent of our sins, and ask Jesus to become our Lord and Savior. The reward is better than a ten-pounder! It is eternity in heaven, the most awesome place God ever created.

**TIP**
Stroking a giant spoon or jig will often trigger big bass to bite.

# SEPTEMBER 17

**HEBREWS 11:26**

*[Moses esteemed] the reproach of Christ greater riches than
the treasures in Egypt. For he looked to the reward.*

When it comes to fishing line, just about every benefit comes with a negative of some sort. Braid is tough and strong with small diameter, but it has no stretch and is harder to cast. Fluorocarbon is pretty invisible under water, but it is unmanageable, stiffer, and breaks unexpectedly. Softer lines are great to fish with but not very abrasion resistant. I could go on.

Life paints lots of pretty pictures of success, but many of those successes could require compromise—saying or doing something we know is immoral and ungodly. There is generally something pulling on us that is attractive or glamorous or that offers money, power, or fame. All we need to do is something we know we shouldn't. What is our solution? Faith—absolutely knowing God has something better for us as we honor Him, praise Him, and thank Him for that greater reward.

**TIP**
Lighter lines allow crankbaits to fish deeper.

JIMMY HOUSTON

REVELATION 22:14

*Blessed are those who do His commandments, that*
*they may have the right to the tree of life.*

My wife, Chris, won the Patoka Lake, Indiana, Bass 'n Gal Tournament by fishing only one tree the second day of the tournament. We called it the magic tree. All 160 competitors in that tournament had the right to fish that tree, but no one else did. Chris knew a secret about that tree that no other woman knew: a school of big bass lived in it. Had the other women known, they would have stood in line to fish that tree.

As you can see in today's verse, God has an even better tree that we all have a right to: the tree of life. The secret to finding it? Obey His commandments. Can we really do that? Not really, but God sent His Son, Jesus, to die on the cross to pay the price for all the times we have broken those commandments. The reward is much greater than the boat Chris won at Patoka!

> **TIP**
> Check your
> line often for
> bad spots.

PROVERBS 30:8

*Remove falsehood and lies far from me; give
me neither poverty or riches.*

Bass tournaments at the top pro level are the perfect example of poverty or riches! Win the tournament and it's $100,000 plus. Miss the money and it is zero dollars. In some events nowadays, everyone gets a check. Truth be known, after the official practice days, where we try to locate fish and fine-tune patterns, most pros don't think they have the fish found to win first place, but pretty much all of them think they can do well enough to cash a smaller check in one of the other places.

In today's verse, Agur was basically asking God to bless him with what we might call a middle-class state in life. The first part is easy—no one wants poverty. The second is actually humbling. Agur did not pray for riches. Wealth can create pride and self-sufficiency that often leaves God out of your life—a sure path to failure.

**TIP**

A bucktail jig will often outproduce rubber skirted jigs as the water cools.

1 PETER 3:7

*Husbands, likewise, dwell with them with understanding, giving honor to the wife.*

At personal appearances around the country, I kid the young girls to not be concerned about guys being cute and cool. After you have been married to the guy for twenty years or so, cute and cool go away. So find you a boy with a bass boat, and if it's a Ranger—even better. For the boys, just find a girl who likes to fish; and if she has a boat, marry her!

> **TIP**
> Count down swimbaits to fish at the proper depth.

I often mention putting God first in all we do. I'm not an expert on marriage, but after more than fifty years married to the same woman, I am an expert on her. Husband, honor your wife in your marriage and she will be thrilled to have you as the leader of the house. You need to be protecting her, providing for her, and being a strength she can always count on. And remember: God Himself is asking you to do this.

# SEPTEMBER 21

**PROVERBS 28:19**

*He who tills his land will have plenty of bread.*

Big crankbaits that dive ten to twenty feet or more catch lots of big bass. They get where the fish live and look like something good for a bass to eat. The problem is, they are lots of work. Throw them all day, and there's a price to pay in sore shoulders, backs, elbows, and wrists. I suggest using a lightweight 6'9"–7'3" rod with medium-heavy action. Your hard work will pay off—and you might just catch dinner.

**TIP**
Round blades produce more vibration.

Today's verse is simply saying work hard, eat well. I believe God wants more out of us than just working. He wants us working exceptionally. Be the best in the office. Be the best at the factory. Be the best working at Bass Pro. Be the best wherever you are and whatever you are doing. God wants you to shine on the job. He has great plans for you that will provide plenty. All we need to do is till our land. God will take over and make our crops flourish.

PSALM 118:25

*Save now I pray, O LORD; O LORD, I pray, send now prosperity.*

My first really big national championship tournament to win was the Project Sports Classic on Amistad Reservoir near Del Rio, Texas. The top fifty in the year's standings qualified for this championship. Chris also finished in the top ten at Amistad. The win paid $6,000! Paltry in today's tournament world, but enormous for us. We made a sizable down payment on a trailer home—not a double-wide, just a single-wide. But talk about prosperity— thank You, Lord! I believe that was in 1967.

It is okay to ask for God's favor and blessing. God has the power to have a sudden impact on your finances, like winning a tournament, getting a great job, or meeting the right person. Go ahead and ask; God will perfectly align things for your benefit. Get ready for God's blessings.

**TIP**
Use shad-colored jerkbaits on clear lakes over deep brush piles (ten to fifteen feet) in late summer and fall.

EXODUS 31:18

*He gave Moses two tablets of the Testimony, tablets of stone, written with the finger of God.*

Rocks are super structures to fish. They provide underwater shady areas, irregular bottom contour, and a good place for moss and algae to grow. This attracts crawfish and other baitfish, which attract bass. Several baits will work, but a crankbait that will bump into the rocks is hard to beat.

God took two rocks, carved them into tablets, and used His finger to write on them. Think about that! No laser, no water saw, just God's almighty finger. We know the Israelites didn't obey and broke that covenant over and over. They had instructions to give them health, wealth, peace, and long life, yet they broke the deal. When we accept Jesus, God takes that same almighty finger and writes on our hearts. His instructions are for our benefit: joy, peace, health, abundance, and more.

**TIP**

A drop shot can be fished on a cast as well as vertically jigged.

### MATTHEW 26:41

*"Watch and pray, lest you enter into temptation. The spirit indeed is willing, but the flesh is weak."*

It is really important to pay attention to what is going on around you at all times while fishing. Watch your line; watch your electronics; look for movement in the water, birds, conditions changing. It is all important as you stay on guard. And praying helps too.

In today's verse, Jesus was talking to Peter, one of His most trusted disciples. He told Peter, as He tells us, how to keep from entertaining temptation, to keep from actually acting on what we are being tempted by. This may mean not going to the wrong places or hanging out with the wrong people. We must be on guard at all times and be on the watch for Satan's tricks. God knows we are weak when tempted. That's why in today's scripture, Jesus added His own personal tip: pray. Next time you are tempted, don't run with the devil; run to God.

**TIP**

Locate roaming schools of bass over deep water with a forward-scanning LiveScope sonar.

EPHESIANS 2:8

*By grace you have been saved through faith, and*
*that not of yourselves; it is the gift of God.*

Vegetation growing to the surface can make farm pond fishing tough this time of the year. Rubber frogs seem to be the best over this vegetation, but a plastic worm rigged Texas-style and weedless works great as well. I like as small a slip sinker as possible and will peg the sinker with a toothpick. With either bait, be sure to pause for about a count of three before setting the hook.

Isn't it fantastic that God doesn't pause and wait awhile when we repent of our sins and ask Him to save us? We don't have to get our act together, prove that we're worthy, or do something beneficial for the church. While we're still dirty and stained by sin, God saves us by His marvelous grace. We haven't earned it and don't deserve it; it's God's gift to us.

**TIP**

A sinking worm, Texas rigged, skips well under docks.

PROVERBS 29:11

*A fool vents all his feelings, but a wise man holds them back.*

We've had lots of pretty silly things happen in bass tournaments when competitors have lost their tempers over fishing holes—arguments over who got there first, and so forth. I've seen them get close to becoming violent, and the fights carry over to the weigh-in, the parking lot, even the next tournament. Once, the pro leading the tournament after two days got so angry with other competitors that he quit fishing, loaded his boat, and went home, missing out on the $100,000 first prize.

God warns that it's not wise to just let it all hang out and say your piece. There are times when our anger rises; it happens. If we're wise, we will zip it up and say nothing. Even when we're cheated, we're hurt, we've been wronged, or we're just upset about something, God's advice is to say nothing and be considered a wise man or a wise woman.

> **TIP**
> Bass can't hear sonar, so leave your fish finders on, but make as little noise as possible in your boat.

2 CHRONICLES 20:20
*Believe in the LORD your God, and you shall be established;*
*believe His prophets, and you shall prosper.*

M any have said that confidence is the best lure in your tackle box. Well, I don't know about that, but I do know you need to believe you're going to catch a fish on the very next cast. Not an hour from now or when the clouds roll in, but *this* cast. Keep believing cast after cast.

Did you know that you can believe your way into success or believe your way into failure? God was not saying you *might* be established or you *might* prosper; God said you *will* prosper. His one requirement is that you believe. How can God promise this? Because He can make it happen. He is not just a God of the natural; our God is supernatural. He can move mountains, create opportunities, redefine your ideas, improve your work habits. Believe you shall prosper!

**TIP**
Use larger buzz baits in choppy water.

### 2 CORINTHIANS 5:21

*He made Him who knew no sin to be sin for us, that we might become the righteousness of God in Him.*

To become better fishermen, we need to try to eliminate the time our lures spend in places where we have little or no chance of catching a fish. Most baits are in places where they can catch fish only 2 to 3 percent of the time. Make shorter casts, use flipping and pitching methods, move closer to your targets, and parallel the bank more. Anyone can double or triple his or her opportunities, but you have to work at it.

We increase our chances of being righteous by 100 percent the second we make Jesus Lord of our lives. All our sins, mistakes, and bad decisions are turned to righteousness. We trade our sins to become the righteousness of God Himself. This is God's plan for you and me: simply repent of your sins and ask Jesus to be your Lord and Savior!

**TIP**

When skipping a lure with spinning reels, feather the line with your index finger.

PROVERBS 3:6

*In all your ways acknowledge Him, and He shall direct your paths.*

**D**o you remember when you first started fishing? Remember how little you knew? Maybe you backlashed a lot and felt lucky, not skilled, when you actually caught a fish. I can't remember when I started fishing; I was maybe two years old. But I sure can remember a lot I couldn't do well. Learning to cast a casting reel was a nightmare. I was the man of constant backlashes.

Have you ever praised God when you backlashed your reel? Actually, you're blessed to have a reel to backlash. It's easy to acknowledge and praise God during the good times, the victories, the abundance, the perfect casts. But here's God's deal for us—acknowledge Him, praise Him, worship Him, even during life's backlashes. He will direct us right out of life's mess-ups. Having a backlash day? Acknowledge and praise God. He will direct you right out of that backlash. Make another cast!

**TIP**

Use a slight pressure to lead fish out from under boat docks. Don't horse 'em!

JIMMY HOUSTON

TITUS 2:12

*Denying ungodliness and worldly lusts, we should live
soberly, righteously, and godly in the present age.*

My buddy Ron Lindner, the brother of Al Lindner, just
went home to heaven. Ron was eighty-six years old
and a great fisherman. I've had lots of comments, emails,
and phone calls about Ron's passing. I will always reply,
"He was a godly man!"

When it's all said and done here in
this life on earth, that's what each of
us should want: to be remembered as
a godly man or a godly woman. We turn
down that drink at a social gathering. When
others would lie, cheat, commit adultery,
we don't. When the world—its pleasures, its
money, its pride, and its power—is placed
first in people's lives, we put God first in
ours. When gossip, bad talk, anger, and
boasting is the norm, we zip it up. We deny
ungodliness even when it's deemed morally
correct. We can live life as godly men or godly women.

**TIP**

Murky water
will generally
clear up quicker
in grassy areas
than in areas
without grass.

OCTOBER

## OCTOBER 1

ROMANS 10:9

*If you confess with your mouth the Lord Jesus and believe in your heart that God has raised Him from the dead, you will be saved.*

F ishing doesn't need to be complicated. It can be extremely simple. All you need is a hook and line and a worm, cricket, or grasshopper to put on the hook. You can go fishing and catch fish!

Salvation, being saved into eternity, as today's scripture says, is just that simple. Even a child can do it. I was saved at twelve years of age. But I could completely understand Jesus loved me. I knew I didn't want to go to hell. I knew I needed to repent of my sins, ask Jesus to forgive them, and invite Him to become Lord of my life. This is salvation at its very simplest. It's as easy as putting a grasshopper on a hook. And it's as rewarding as living an abundant life here on earth and eternity in heaven.

**TIP**

Large square-bill crankbaits will produce even in shallow water.

MATTHEW 5:16

*Let your light so shine before men, that they may see your good works and glorify your Father in heaven.*

The coldest practice day I can remember was at Smith Lake, Alabama. Chris and I were staying with our longtime friend Red Berry. On practice days, Red would launch us at daylight on a private ramp and load us back out at dark. On the second day of practice, it was only 12 degrees Fahrenheit. The last thing Red said was, "If y'all get too cold, call me and I'll be right here!" Chris gave me one of those looks as I told Red, "We'll see you at dark!" On the final tournament day, with only two fish in the live well, I eased my boat into my last spot with thirty minutes left to fish, caught two nice bass, and with under a minute to go, caught my last keeper. As I stood onstage, praising God for that last thirty minutes and a $10,000 check, God was glorified because of Red Berry's good works. How could you be glorified because of your kindness today? Show kindness and see!

**TIP**
Fish will suspend under floating docks.

# OCTOBER 3

## GENESIS 5:27
*All the days of Methuselah were nine hundred*
*and sixty-nine years; and he died.*

After fifty-four years of national tournament fishing, we decided not to fish the 2020 season. We picked a good year not to fish. I may go back. Honestly, I miss the people more than the competition. Many thought I would die in the front of a bass boat. And I still might. But it probably won't be in a tournament.

Do you know how the man most famous for being the oldest man to ever live died? I don't either, but I believe that after 969 years of living, he died in the flood. I ciphered it out. The flood left only eight humans alive, the rest being destroyed by God. As long as Methuselah lived, it's a drop in the minnow bucket to eternity! That's what God has promised you and me—eternity with Jesus in heaven.

**TIP**
When targeting individual structures, only fish a foot or so around your target.

### MATTHEW 4:4

*"It is written, 'Man shall not live by bread alone, but by
every word that proceeds from the mouth of God.'"*

If we could talk to fish, how good could we become as
fishermen? I'd really like to interview mama largemouth. *What color spinnerbait is your favorite?
Would you have bitten a worm if I had
thrown that? Where do you go after a cold
front? Can you see my fishing line?* It
would be an awfully long interview.

Well, we can interview God! We can
learn all about Him just by reading His
Word. Plus, we can find out how God
would react in every situation. That's what
Jesus was doing in today's scripture as He
was resisting Satan's temptations. Guess
what: Satan will tempt us often, just as
he did Jesus. We are armed with the same
weapon Jesus used to resist that temptation. Keep God's
Word close by, in your heart and mind. It will work for
you as well.

**TIP**
Match your
tube and other
soft plastic to
the color of
bait the fish
are eating.

1 PETER 3:4

*Rather let [your adornment] be the hidden person of the
heart, with the incorruptible beauty of a gentle and quiet
spirit, which is very precious in the sight of God.*

I was taking pictures of my daughter, Sherri, with a really big buck she had taken when she said, "Wouldn't you know it? I don't have any makeup on!" I remember at Bass 'n Gal tournaments the first thing most girls did after checking in, before they took their bass out of the live wells, was reach for the lipstick, hairbrush, mirror, and those little powder puff things.

In today's verse, Peter was talking about how God sees beauty in wives and what is the most special to Him: the beauty that lasts forever and can't be corrupted even by wind, rain, sun, and storm for you fishing gals. It is a beautiful, quiet, and gentle spirit. That beauty is a gift from God for the benefit of us husbands and everyone else.

**TIP**

A falling tide will usually draw crawfish out of rocks and riprap, which turns the bass bite on.

EZEKIEL 36:27

*"I will put My Spirit within you and cause you to walk in My statutes, and you will keep My judgments and do them."*

Occasionally, something will happen while fishing that will cause us to completely change what we're doing. Did you ever have a crankbait tangle up on a cast, come spinning back to the boat on top the water, and see a bass blow up on it? *Bingo*. Let's change to a topwater. And work it fast.

In today's scripture, we see how getting saved completely changes us. God was prophesying through Ezekiel to the children of Israel about what added spiritual blessing they would receive upon returning from captivity. This still hasn't happened. Most Jews in Israel still don't believe in Jesus. But I do! I'm praying you do too. Because we have God's Spirit in us, our daily goal is to let His Spirit lead, walk in His laws, and obey them continually.

**TIP**

On dual-axle trailers, a ramp works better than a jack to elevate the trailer.

HEBREWS 11:1

*Faith is the substance of things hoped for,*
*the evidence of things not seen.*

As we learn more about fishing, we begin to rely on certain baits under different types of conditions. A spinnerbait on cloudy and windy days. Topwater early in the morning. Suspended jerkbaits in late winter on clear lakes. Jigs in thick, heavy bushes. I could go on and on. We're not positive we'll catch a bass on these lures at these times, but we think we will. This is faith in a fishing lure.

If we can have faith in a fishing lure, how can we not have faith in the God who hung the stars, made blind eyes see, raised paralyzed people to walk, and brought the dead back to life? This Jesus walked on water, sacrificed His holy body and then His holy life to pay the price for your sins and mine, and walked out of that grave alive! I have that faith, that victory. Do you?

**TIP**
Bass will follow the water in as a lake rises.

PSALM 119:173

*Let Your hand become my help, for I have chosen Your precepts.*

Breakdowns of some sort happen every day in tournament fishing. The good thing is, competitors are always ready to help one another. Flag down the next boat that comes by and you have help. Tournaments have been won due to a helping hand.

How do we come boldly before almighty God and ask for His help? By choosing to live by His guidelines—not ours, not the world's. When we are honoring God and putting Him first in all we do, we know God wants to help. And when God helps, amazing things begin to happen. What could never happen in the natural happens by the supernatural power of God. Doors begin to open. Health improves. Addictions cease. We meet the right people. Start getting the right breaks. We can dial up God's help today just by living by His precepts.

**TIP**
As it gets colder, shad will group in tighter balls and love to hang around the mouths of creeks.

# OCTOBER 9

1 THESSALONIANS 4:11

*Aspire to lead a quiet life, to mind your own business, and to work with your own hands.*

**M**y fishing and hunting buddy George Cochran from Hot Springs was a super tournament fisherman. He won both the Bassmaster Classic and the FLW Forrest Wood Cup Championship. His nickname is Gentleman George. As talented as George was in competition, as funny as he was onstage talking about fishing and hunting, you never saw George in others' affairs.

God loves a man or woman living the simple life. Not a busybody or gossip, but one working hard at whatever tasks lie before him or her. When we do this, God will favor us, bless us, look at us with a smile in His heart! If we get a chance today to say something bad about someone or spread a little gossip, let's just not do that. Pretty quickly, we'll be hearing something good from God.

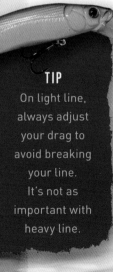

**TIP**

On light line, always adjust your drag to avoid breaking your line. It's not as important with heavy line.

HEBREWS 1:14

*Are they not all ministering spirits sent forth to*
*minister for those who will inherit salvation?*

Topwater baits can be fished at a variety of speeds.
It's up to us to figure out the best speed. One often
overlooked speed is fast—really fast. On a popping bait,
as well as a walking topwater, this amounts to some-
where between working the bait and just
winding it back in. Yes, that fast. I
believe the fish just think it's trying
to escape.

Today's verse is speaking of something
else really fast: angels. We believe angels
were created to glorify and worship God, the
heavenly host beautifully singing praises to
Him. And I guess they were. They are sent
here to us not to preach but to minister, to
help, encourage, save from danger, to guide
us and brighten our paths. I don't know how
many are assigned to each of us, but I'm
pretty sure God has had to send reinforcements to me at
times! I imagine that could be true for you as well.

**TIP**
Windy days
will draw
bass from
deep to
shallow on
rocky banks.

# OCTOBER 11

MATTHEW 11:28

*"Come to Me, all you who labor and are heavy*
*laden, and I will give you rest."*

A few baits lend themselves to just being dragged along the bottom—a Carolina rig (a weight on a swivel with a few feet of line behind the weight, and a hook baited with soft plastics, such as lizards), a shaky head jig with a smaller plastic on it, or a Ned rig.

Dragging fishing lures is productive. Dragging past sins is not. These sins are forgiven once we are saved. They are completely forgotten by God. When someone reminds you of them, tell that individual, "Those sins are gone forever. That's not who I am." You are a brand-new man or woman of God, fully justified, forgiven and made holy by the blood of Jesus. You're no longer carrying that heavy load of lying, cheating, addiction, adultery, or anything else. God will carry you higher than you could ever imagine.

**TIP**

On bright, clear days, a frog with a yellow belly seems to work well, especially if bluegill are present.

LUKE 12:40

*"You also be ready, for the Son of Man is coming at an hour you do not expect."*

When we learn the places bass return to throughout the year, year after year, we can catch more fish. Before and after the spawn, bass stage in points, docks, and trees. In the fall they use the same places. Many folks dial back on fishing from September through the colder months. They're missing some of the best fishing trips of the year. Lakes are less crowded, and falling water temps make bass more active.

Jesus said He was coming back to earth. He's coming to claim His chosen. We don't want to miss out; we want to be ready. This is our immediate trip to heaven. This is the day the dead in Christ come out of their graves and join the Lord in heaven. What a glorious day and sight that will be. But what a terror-filled day that will be for those unsaved, those lost and left behind. Be ready. I'm ready.

**TIP**
Sound travels about four times faster in water than through the air.

# OCTOBER 13

PSALM 119:135
*Make Your face shine upon Your servant, and teach me Your statutes.*

W hen you fish all over the country, you really have to pay attention to state laws (statutes). Even here in Oklahoma we have different laws about fish length and number limits on several lakes.

We need to know and keep God's laws too. Why? Because they're for our benefit. It doesn't really benefit God for us to keep His statutes. It helps us. How can we benefit in the long haul by lying, cheating, stealing, committing adultery, coveting, disrespecting our parents, or killing? Honestly, we can't—and this list could fill the page. On the flip side, if God's face is shining down on us, amazing things happen. Doors open. Breaks happen. We meet the right people. Things meant to harm us instead help us. God's grace and goodness start flowing through our lives. Keep obeying and watch blessings shine down in abundance. Our God is shining.

**TIP**
A HydroWave sound machine seems to work best when using the delayed playback mode.

### TITUS 2:6

*Likewise, exhort the young men to be sober-minded.*

I t is important when fishing shallow water to learn to make a soft landing with your lure, not a big splash that might spook a fish enough to keep it from biting. We do this by making a cast low to the water, slowing the bait down, and stopping it just before it hits the water. No splash, just a parting of the water. Today's verse teaches young people how to part the waters of life.

**TIP**
Always use O-rings on wacky rigs.

The apostle Paul was teaching Titus what and how to instruct young Christians: how to live in such a way that they were perfect examples to friend and foe alike. Our lives should be shining examples of what living for God is all about. Folks should know we take God seriously. We should be models of good deeds and integrity. Do this with joy, and people will want to become like us and have what we have: Jesus!

1 JOHN 3:18

*My little children, let us not love in word or*
*in tongue, but in deed and in truth.*

In the fall and early winter, bass can be easy to catch, especially when they hit the banks to fill up on shad. Generally we can crank small square-bills or medium diving crankbaits and whack 'em. Another super technique is stroking a lipless crankbait. We let that bait fall on a tight line, then stroke our rod tip up high. This dropping and stroking action catches fish. But trust me: it's a lot of work!

It takes some work to show God's love too. It's easy to talk a good game, but it's another to put that love into action by doing a good deed for someone else. In this day and time, it is so much easier to give a little money and let someone else do the work. Remember, God knows your heart. Do something good for someone today.

**TIP**
Add Mylar reflective strips of red or yellow to enhance the color on spoons.

ZECHARIAH 9:12

*Return to the stronghold, you prisoners of hope. Even*
*today I declare that I will restore double to you.*

It's very cool to catch two fish at once. We do it quite a bit crappie fishing with two crappie baits. It's relatively easy fishing for white bass or stripers with multiple lures. I actually caught three largemouth bass, a three-, four-, and six-pounder, on an Alabama rig. That was really special!

In today's verse, God was telling His chosen people, the children of Israel, that He was about to pay them back double. Think about that. When bad happens to us, we have just qualified for double restoration. When people cheat you, steal from you, fire you, God is waiting to pay you back double. Remember Job? Even when the dam explodes on your lake (that one is personal), God is ready, willing, and perfectly able to pay us back double. And He will.

**TIP**
During winter, the clearer the water, the deeper the fish will be.

## PHILIPPIANS 4:19

*My God shall supply all your need according to His riches in glory by Christ Jesus.*

On a recent trip to Rockport, Texas, we fished with guide and owner of the Lodge at Goose Island, Brett Phillips. We caught lots of redfish and black drum every single trip out. The key, in addition to Brett's expertise, was a really good air boat he supplied that allowed us to fish places other fishermen simply could not fish. He supplied everything to give us a great trip.

God has promised to supply us with everything we need to live an abundant life. We really don't have to fret or worry about the perfect job, the right timing, or meeting the right people. God already has that in the bank for us and will supply it at just the right time. My belief is that God has it all and has an abundance of blessings set aside for you and me. Much more than we will ever need.

**TIP**
Spend a couple of hours every fishing trip trying a new technique or one you don't often fish.

HEBREWS 12:1

*Let us run with endurance the race that is set before us.*

Years ago, B.A.S.S. had the brilliant idea that we should combine bass-fishing tournaments and bass boat racing. After all, we all loved to race and had bass boats that would practically fly. B.A.S.S. tried it in a couple of tournaments, but it went over like a lead balloon as a serious competition for the public. I've got to admit, though—all the competitors loved it.

Two things grab me in today's verse. One is that we need to each run our own race God has given us. Don't worry about someone else's race. We won't all run the race of an MLB player or NBA star, a preacher, or a president. God gave you and me our own special races. The second is, we have to give it all we've got and never give up. Jesus ran His race knowing the finish line was the cross. Walking out of that grave was the victory; eternity and heaven, the prize. Let's race!

**TIP**
Fish often suspend out away from the bank in late fall.

GALATIANS 3:26
*You are all sons of God through faith in Christ Jesus.*

Sometimes we find fish by figuring out where they are not. That's usually easier than figuring out where they are. Pros call this eliminating water. The more knowledge we have, the more water we eliminate before we even launch our boats. Often, that allows us to go directly to the fish.

God has equipped us to eliminate many bad situations in life. Not everyone uses what He supplies. Isn't it awesome to realize you are a son or daughter of God Himself! Realize also that we need to live like God's sons and daughters. We need to hold our heads up and realize that no matter what, our Father has our backs. He loves us with an unconditional love. He has the power and resources to take care of and fix any problems we have. Tackle life today knowing your Father can eliminate any bad situation you encounter! Stand tall, son or daughter of God.

**TIP**
Work your bait differently on different casts to figure the cadence, rhythm, and speed fish want.

ISAIAH 43:25

*"I, even I, am He who blots out your transgressions for*
*My own sake; and I will not remember your sins."*

With the advanced electronics we have today, do we still need marker buoys? Marker buoys, of course, are small floating buoys, usually brightly colored, with a line and weight attached to mark a spot. Most spots now are marked with waypoints on a GPS. I combine old technology and new by immediately tossing a marker overboard when I catch a fish in open water. I then peruse all around that buoy with my LiveScope looking for structures and fish.

When we ask Jesus to be our Lord and Savior, God never puts a buoy or waypoint on our sins. His GPS page of us is completely clean. The blood of Jesus has deleted all our sin, past, present, and future. God did all that for His own sake and benefit, but it's even more beneficial to us. Grace—it's amazing!

**TIP**

Slowly trolling jerkbaits in clear-water lakes can be an excellent school locator and can also help you catch giant bass in the winter.

## MATTHEW 10:32

*"Whoever confesses Me before men, him I will also confess before My Father who is in heaven."*

For years, I worked the FLW Fun Zone on Saturdays and Sundays if I didn't make the top twenty. I worked for Shell, Quaker State, Rotella, and our other sponsors. My job was to meet with fans, sign autographs, take pics, answer questions, and so forth. Several other competitors did the same. Many, however, just gathered together and talked fishing for hours, about what they did or didn't do in the tournament. Why did they do this? Some to learn, some to just brag on themselves. But they all had a love and passion for bass fishing.

Shouldn't we be talking about Jesus for hours too? Are we just shy, or are we embarrassed? Are we proud of Jesus, or ashamed? Let's confess Jesus today. Let's brag on Jesus every chance we get. And Jesus will brag on us.

**TIP**
Even when it's cold, some bass will always move shallow on warm afternoons.

PSALM 8:5

*You have made [man] a little lower than the angels,*
*and You have crowned him with glory and honor.*

It's difficult to attain a big name in professional bass fishing. How do guys like Hank Parker, Roland Martin, Bill Dance, Ricky Clunn, or Kevin VanDam become household names to almost any fisherman? Sure, they are extraordinary fishermen with extraordinary talents and skills. Sure, they win and do well often, but they have also taken those God-given talents and moved them to the max. They've added a sparkle and flair that makes them magnetic. They set themselves apart from the field and became exceptional.

> **TIP**
> Forward-looking sonar is needed to spot rocks and stumps in front of your boat.

Angels are awesome, mighty beings able to slay thousands. Yet God made you and me just a bit lower than them. He gave us glory, honor, talents, abilities, and gifts that allow us to become exceptional in life. Let's go out there and take them to the max. Let's become exceptional.

JOHN 11:26

*"Whoever lives and believes in Me shall never die. Do you believe this?"*

This is the time of the year when most outdoorsmen have to make a difficult decision: *Do I hunt today, or do I go fishing?* Non-outdoors types don't feel sorry for us, I promise. The biggest problem is, to be really successful, we need to hunt all day or fish all day. Most days, I try to do both on the same day if that's possible. And generally I fail at both on those days.

With God, it is an either-or. Not both. We believe in Jesus or we don't. This statement by Jesus to Martha in today's verse came during the miraculous story when Jesus raised Lazarus from the dead. Seconds before, He told Martha, "I am the resurrection and the life. He who believes in Me, though he may die, he shall live" (John 11:25). This is the question Jesus continues to ask you and me. Do you believe? Yes, Lord, I believe.

**TIP**

You can drill holes in the sides of big spoons and add extra hooks with O-rings.

1 JOHN 3:3

*Everyone who has this hope in Him purifies himself, just as He is pure.*

The difference between underhand casting and pitching is really not too big. Perhaps pitching was developed by folks who couldn't learn to underhand cast or even flip very well. You can become more accurate flipping, but you can make much longer throws casting underhanded and still have superb accuracy.

Casting underhanded is very effective. Living underhanded is not. God wants us living our lives pure. We think of some businesspeople as being underhanded. Politicians and lawyers are often described that way. People lose their purity generally by compromise, which usually happens a little at a time. After a while, we become a good distance from pure. We may say or do something we would never have considered a few months or years ago. Jesus never compromised. He remained pure. Let's do our best to follow His example.

**TIP**

As the water gets cold, below fifty degrees, start slowly dragging baits on the bottom.

1 THESSALONIANS 4:14
*If we believe that Jesus died and rose again, even so God*
*will bring with Him those who sleep in Jesus.*

Fishing around mayflies is exciting, especially for blue-gill, but bass hang around a good mayfly hatch as well. Mayflies are amazing little creatures. The female lays her eggs on the water; then they sink to the bottom or attach to vegetation and become nymphs that live in the water about a year. These nymphs come to the surface and hatch into mayflies, which live only a few hours, maybe a day!

The mayfly, created by God, lives almost all of its life underwater, but it is alive and flying into the air right before it mates and dies. If God can create the amazing mayfly, He can and certainly will raise our bodies to unite with our souls in heaven when Jesus returns. Those still alive have that one-way flight with Jesus straight to heaven, body and soul.

**TIP**
Use live bait to catch really huge bass.

DEUTERONOMY 8:18

*You shall remember the LORD your God, for it is*
*He who gives you power to get wealth.*

I've heard it said many times about some superstar tournament angler, "He's forgotten more than I'll ever know." You'll never hear me say that. I've fished with these guys; they don't forget anything!

Today's verse bothers many Christians. Some think you have to be poor and suffer to be a good Christian. Even wealthy Christians feel guilty at times. But God creates wealth. This magnificent story started with God telling Abraham He would give him and his descendants hundreds of thousands, maybe even millions of acres of land. And He did. Does that sound like a God who wants you and me poor and suffering? I think not. Not every Christian will become financially wealthy, but every Christian will be richly blessed. Remember the Lord your God; put Him first in all you do. Expect His blessings.

**TIP**
Always have a rod handy with a good schooling fish bait in the fall.

EPHESIANS 3:14

*For this reason I bow my knees to the Father of our Lord Jesus Christ.*

Although many people use these early winter months to locate, see, and ultimately catch giant bass, finesse baits still produce bites throughout the cold winter months. On clear lakes, tiny sixteenth- and thirty-second–ounce finesse jig heads with tiny hooks and one to three inches of soft plastic produce almost any time. No added action needed. Just let them fall and retrieve. You may not catch giants, but the reason we fish is to catch fish.

The reason we worship God is to ultimately get to heaven. God has prepared a permanent home for us. But we also worship God because He is the God of the impossible here on earth. He's able to take our most dire circumstances and turn them into a blessing, our setbacks into step-ups, and our failures into victories. I bow my knees and can't wait to see what God is doing next in my life.

**TIP**

Tighten your drag down when fishing for bass in heavy cover.

JIMMY HOUSTON

PROVERBS 11:27

*He who earnestly seeks good finds favor, but*
*trouble will come to him who seeks evil.*

Fishing is definitely a grown-up's game of hide-and-seek. Sure, modern electronics have helped tremendously, but we still have those desperate times when we can't locate fish. I've said often, point jumping has bailed me out many times. Ironically, just the opposite works as well—fishing the tail ends of pockets. Again, go from pocket to pocket, fishing only the very tail end of each one.

**TIP**
Calm water generally requires longer casts.

Finding God is a much easier task. Obviously, we see the hand of God and His works all around us. We find Him by talking with Him and reading His Word. We seek God by praying and praying often. The more we read God's Word, the closer He comes to us. God is always at our fingertips. We just need to reach out and take His hand. When you do, get ready! God is about to release His favor and enormous blessings.

DEUTERONOMY 3:22
*You must not fear them, for the LORD your God Himself fights for you.*

One of the keys to catching fish consistently is to fish our strengths most of the day. In other words, do what we do best. It might be working with a certain bait, such as a spinnerbait, worm, or crankbait we are better with or have more confidence in. It could be a technique like flipping or drop shotting. We may be better offshore than at casting accuracy. Fish your strengths.

In today's verse, Moses was recalling what he told Joshua before Joshua set out to conquer the promised land. We serve that same God. Whatever enemy we have, God will fight for us. God is our strength. The enemy might be drugs, alcohol, lying, cheating, health problems, or many other things. The enemy may be the devil himself! It doesn't matter; we need not fear. God will defeat our enemies. He's fighting our battles right now.

**TIP**
Fish faster-moving baits right before a cold front.

PROVERBS 14:23

*In all labor there is profit, but idle chatter leads only to poverty.*

Fishing is all about telling stories. Some call them fish tales. Some call them outright lies purely made up! While most of that is all in fun, when the tournament starts, it's all business. It's all work. Idle chatter doesn't win tournament money. As talkative as I am, I hardly say much during competition.

In the South, we would paraphrase idle chatter as sitting around shooting the bull. And we do that a lot, but not while working. God wants us working. God wants us accomplishing. And He says there is gain for us when we labor. Remember that profit is not always financial. Many times, it's just knowing a job is well done. Sometimes it's becoming a better person. But always, we profit. Let's go to work.

**TIP**
Run eight-gauge wire to your LiveScope transducer to help eliminate interference.

MATTHEW 13:58

*He did not do many mighty works there because of their unbelief.*

It is so easy to get discouraged fishing. Most kids often give up after just a few minutes fishing if they don't catch one. Some adults are pretty much the same. The trick is, you've got to believe you're going to catch one on the very next cast. I believe I'm going to catch one every cast. Is this belief easy? Of course not. But we must do it to fight through all the casts that come home empty-handed.

This verse tells me we must believe in order for Jesus to do mighty works in our lives. Our unbelief actually holds God back from performing miracles and blessing our socks off. While Jesus was here, folks repeatedly said, "Prove it!" Jesus consistently admonished, "Do you believe? Do you trust?" What are you telling God today? "Prove it," or "I believe"? Let's not hold God back. Let's believe and unleash miracles.

TIP
When tournament fishing, always use a trailer hook on a spinnerbait.

NOVEMBER

# NOVEMBER 1

### JAMES 1:4
*Let patience have its perfect work, that you may*
*be perfect and complete, lacking nothing.*

A s water cools off more and more, jerkbaits play a bigger part in our arsenal of baits. We also move from the floating jerkbaits used in the summer to more suspended models, like we used in February. The more patient we are, the more strikes we will get. When you stop that suspended jerkbait, let it set as long as you can . . . and then let it set some more! Should patience be working in every Christian? I think it should. As we grow in Christ, we should become more patient with everyone around us and more patient with ourselves. This patience causes us to become better Christians, more like Christ. Having trouble with patience? Remember how patient God has been and still is with most of us. He's patient enough to forgive every sin while we grow.

**TIP**
Most bass are caught in ten feet of water and shallower!

PSALM 73:3

*I was envious of the boastful, when I saw the prosperity of the wicked.*

We all know fishing is about bragging. We all do it. Ever catch an eight- or ten-pound bass and not take a picture of it? Only when you didn't have a camera! This bragging is good; it's fun; it's healthy. We are sharing in another's excitement and success. We're not envious at all. But what about when we see evil succeed, when we see the wicked prosper? How do we feel about some big-head fisherman who brags constantly and wins?

The entire seventy-third psalm talks about just that. We know envy is a sin. But it's really difficult not to be envious of the ungodly, who seem to be prospering while we struggle, until we realize what we have in God is worth more than all the world offers. Rest assured, God will strike the wicked and reward the righteous. Jesus has made us righteous.

**TIP**
Search out old, broken-down boat docks for the best crappie and bass fishing.

JOB 8:21

*He will yet fill your mouth with laughing,*
*and your lips with rejoicing.*

One of the really tough tournaments for Chris was the 1977 Bass 'n Gal Classic on Lake Ferguson, a navigable oxbow lake off the Mississippi River. Chris was catching a few but certainly not enough to win. On the final day, her dear friend and fellow competitor Freda Adams told her, "I'm getting bites fishing between the parked barges but can't catch them, and I can't get my spinnerbait in between the barges very well."

Chris immediately switched to a lure she could accurately cast far back between the barges. Chris won that Bass 'n Gal Classic!

Today's verse has Job's friend trying to reassure him. No matter how bad things are (and life was horrible for Job for a time), God has better plans for us. He has rejoicing. So keep praising God. He will not leave you, and, like Job, you may receive double.

**TIP**

Don't be afraid to fish really deep for wintertime spotted bass, even more than forty feet deep.

PROVERBS 16:7

*When a man's ways please the LORD, He makes*
*even his enemies to be at peace with him.*

Nothing pleases us more than catching a fish exactly where we thought the fish should be. How many times have we all said, "She came right out from under that log" or "right off the corner of that dock" or "just when my bait hit that brush pile!" We like it because our knowledge is paying off. We knew there should be a fish on that spot.

We know exactly how to act to please God. Today's verse tells how happy God is when our ways line up with what He likes. He's so happy, He will cause even our enemies to love us and help us. If our enemies are evil, God may take what they have and give it to us. Isn't that wild? Let's live today to please God and watch Him change folks around us for our benefit.

**TIP**
Move to smaller willow leaf blades in clearer, cooling water.

MATTHEW 6:14

*"If you forgive men their trespasses, your heavenly Father will also forgive you."*

I received a note on social media from a gentleman who said he and I had a major disagreement at a show in Sacramento back in the eighties. He said he had held a grudge against me ever since, but his attitude had changed. In real life, our not forgiving hurts us more than the one who hurt us. Funny thing is, I've never been to Sacramento!

Forgiving is essential in Christianity. We trust God to forgive us when we ask. We are lost without His forgiveness, but it's about the hardest thing in the world to forgive someone who has really hurt us, really done us wrong. In today's verse Jesus was speaking, and in the next verse He said if you don't forgive, neither will your Father in heaven forgive your trespasses. Jesus paid the ultimate price to pay for our sins. We are required to forgive those who sin against us.

**TIP**

When water temperatures fall below 50 degrees Fahrenheit, fish a jigging spoon.

LEVITICUS 19:11

*"You shall not steal, nor deal falsely, nor lie to one another."*

How do we go about trying to catch fish? We try to use a line a fish can't see. We make long casts. We slip around quietly and use lures that often look better than the real thing. All to trick a fish into biting that hook, which we try to hide. The better we trick the fish, the more fish we fool into biting.

Do we do this with God—try to trick Him? You don't think this applies to you and me? Have you ever called in sick and not really been too sick to work? Ever kept the incorrect change a clerk accidentally gave you? Fudged on your taxes? Have you misstated your child's age to get a lower price or driven over the speed limit? We've all broken man's rules and God's rules as well. These little sins are important to God. Unrepented of and unforgiven, they lead to bigger sins and more condemnation.

**TIP**
Always mark and fish any underwater rock piles.

NOVEMBER 7

HEBREWS 13:6
*We may boldly say: "The LORD is my helper; I*
*will not fear. What can man do to me?"*

What is the biggest help you have on a bass boat to help you catch fish? Many would quickly say electronics. How about a trolling motor or that big engine on the back? Power Poles, HydroWave, batteries? Must be the rod—no, the lures. The truth is, the best help you have in that boat is . . . you. That's right. Being equipped with all the goodies is beneficial, but you have to use these tools, make the cast, and catch the fish.

God has equipped each of us with all we need to succeed. And anytime we think we fall short on what's needed, God is right there to help. With God helping we succeed regardless of the odds or what people say or think about us. God helps heal. God opens doors. God places the right people in place for us. Need help? Call on your Helper today.

1 JOHN 1:9

*If we confess our sins, He is faithful and just to forgive us*
*our sins and to cleanse us from all unrighteousness.*

Stickups are single pieces of wood structure that stick up above the water's surface. It has nothing to do with the Wild West! These stickups hold fish, particularly on flats and near points. There could be a brush pile under a single, tiny stickup. When you find stickups, fish them all. Spinnerbaits and square-bill cranks usually work well on stickups.

TIP
Move to larger blades as the water cools.

A small sin is like a stickup. It might have a much bigger sin lurking just under the surface. Little sins, white lies, gossip, pride—all these can lead to bigger sins and huge problems. A careless or discouraging word can do more damage than we can ever imagine—and certainly more than we intended. The good thing is God can forgive and cleanse us of those little sins and erase them to keep them from doing damage and growing into bigger problems.

# NOVEMBER 9

PROVERBS 18:21

*Death and life are in the power of the tongue,*
*and those who love it will eat its fruit.*

When the heavens open up and the rain pours down, most fishermen head for cover. Heavy rains ruin a lot of fishing trips. But to many bass anglers, the rain is very welcome. The clouds produce lower light, making the bass less spooky; and generally the barometer is falling. This increases the size of the strike zone, making bass move farther to strike our baits. It's spinnerbait time!

Like heavy rain, our words have the immense power of the greatest good and the greatest bad. Relationships can be damaged beyond repair by ill-chosen words. Fortunes have been lost (and won) by words. Wars have been fought. Lives have been lost. How do we control our tongues? From the heart. If we keep all the good things of God in our hearts, life will proceed from our tongues.

**TIP**

Windy shorelines hold shad, bass, and white bass in the fall.

MATTHEW 25:23

*"His lord said to him, 'Well done, good and faithful servant.'"*

It's stunning when you stand on a stage and hear the announcer say your name, followed by "Your tournament champion!" Or to hear, "Welcome to the stage, this year's B.A.S.S. Angler of the Year!" Very few pro anglers experience that many times, and some never hear it with their names attached.

Today's verse of praise is part of a story Jesus told about servants left in charge of some of their master's money. One had five talents and doubled that amount. The master was elated and put him in charge of more. (These talents were a specific weight of gold or silver and not gifts or abilities.) God has also given each of us money to be a steward of in this life. Some more, some less. While tithing is hardly mentioned in the New Testament, this story tells me Jesus is interested in what we do with our money. We must use it wisely and be called good and faithful servants.

**TIP**
Fish buzzbaits on these nice fall afternoons.

## NOVEMBER 11

1 CORINTHIANS 10:31
*Whether you eat or drink, or whatever you
do, do all to the glory of God.*

Can you remember fishing with a cane pole, a bobber or float with a minnow or worm on your hook, catching crappie, bluegill, or anything else that would bite? Most of today's younger fishermen have never experienced that, and I think they should. I still love the thrill of watching that bobber go under and that special feeling of pulling that fish out with a cane pole. Yet however we are fishing, our goal is to catch fish.

Our daily goal as we walk though this life is to honor God in all we do. Our work, our play, every step of the way, living our lives to the glory of God. By living this way, we don't let little trials and missteps turn into bigger problems. Our relationship with Jesus is closer and stronger. This allows God to touch us with His favor.

**TIP**
Make multiple casts to a piece of structure after a cold front.

PSALM 103:2

*Bless the LORD, O my soul, and forget not all His benefits.*

We are entering the season to begin catching big bass again. I'm talking huge bass: seven, eight, nine pounds—even double-digit bass! Our best tools are modern electronics and big baits. As in geometry, remember this formula: big baits = big bass. After all, those huge bass are used to eating big bluegill, crappie, crawfish, and even other bass well over a pound in size.

We should use big baits to catch big bass, and we should bless God with all we've got from the depths of our souls: big praise for a big God. We bless God when we wake up, and we should still be singing His praises when we hit the hay. We bless the Lord because He saved us and has forgiven our sins. He has redeemed our lives from destruction. When God looks at us, He sees crowns of righteousness sitting high on our heads. *Bless the Lord, O my soul.*

**TIP**
Small bottom variations are more important in shallow lakes.

EZEKIEL 36:26

*"I will give you a new heart and put a new spirit within you."*

I have a fishing buddy and business associate who has a new heart. His original heart was worn-out! He had a heart transplant and received a new heart from a much younger person. A tragedy turned into a blessing. The new heart is amazing, and more amazing is that God made the new heart even better than the first one!

God doesn't reach in, take out our hearts, and stick in new ones, although He could. (Remember what He did with Adam's rib.) God changes our cold, stone-hard hearts to warm, godly hearts of flesh—hearts wanting to do God's will.

Ever wonder why you feel uncomfortable when your buddies use God's name in vain? Wonder why you don't enjoy some of the things you did before? Even some of the people? You have a new heart—a godly heart—a heart designed for greatness.

**TIP**

Try trolling to locate schools of bass, white bass, and crappie.

1 CORINTHIANS 12:7
*The manifestation of the Spirit is given to each one for the profit of all.*

There are all kinds of lures, and all are made to catch fish! Well, they're made to catch fishermen first because the fish don't have any money. But each lure category has available variety to make them work well under different conditions. Take crankbaits: they are made to fish at many depths. Square-bills are for fishing through brush. Cranks come in big, medium, and small. You can find every color, and they even come noisy or quiet.

And that's something like what the manifestation of the Spirit does for us believers. It manifests different gifts to each of us. Some are given wisdom by the Spirit. Some are given knowledge, others more faith. The Spirit gives the power to heal, the words to prophesy or to exhort others, the power to give service. None of us gets all these gifts by the Spirit, but we all benefit from these gifts. Which gifts do you have?

**TIP**
Go as far up in creeks and pockets as you can in both early spring and late fall.

CATCH A BETTER LIFE | 333

JOHN 10:17

*"My Father loves Me, because I lay down*
*My life that I may take it again."*

Laydowns are trees that have fallen in the water but
are still attached to the shore. Some have been cut
by adventurous bass anglers. We have always called my
buddy Roland Martin "Chainsaw." Enough said. Fish
the deep end of the laydown first
while establishing a pattern; then
carefully fish each junction area
on that laydown. It's a terrific structure to
catch them!

In today's verse, Jesus was talking
about a different type of laydown. He
was telling the people about His upcom-
ing death on the cross, when He would
lay down his life. In the next verse, Jesus
said God had told His Son to lay down
His life willingly because God had given Jesus the power
to take it up again. Jesus trusted His Father and did just
that. He walked out of the grave by that power. That
same power is available to you and me. Trust Him!

**TIP**
Lighter line
adds more
action to small
crankbaits
and jigs.

1 PETER 2:9

*You are a chosen generation, a royal priesthood,*
*a holy nation, His own special people.*

This is the time of year to prepare wintertime crappie holes that you can fish from the shore. I search out bluff-type areas on lakes like Tenkiller and Grand here in Oklahoma, Table Rock in Missouri, and Beaver in Arkansas. Seed the bluff areas with cedar to attract and hold crappie. If you find a shelf on these bluffs, drop these cedars to the bottom. If not, suspend the trees at various depths with wire. These special places will hold crappie all winter. They are special because we created them—we put in the brush to attract the fish.

**TIP**
Use a double hook in place of a treble to fish heavy cover with cranks.

God created us. He put the beat in our hearts and chose us to be His. Shouldn't we live our lives as that royal priesthood? We need to be praising God, every day, letting our lives and conduct glorify God. We are special!

PSALM 90:12

*Teach us to number our days, that we may gain a heart of wisdom.*

As we grow older, we begin to lose many friends. We've lost fishing icons and great friends like Ricky Green; Forrest Wood; Ron Linder; my own dad, Jack Houston; and many more. It always hurts and continues to hurt. It's meant to be that way. Included in the legacies these folks leave behind is their great wisdom. I've always known wisdom comes with age. We don't get any smarter, but we do get wiser.

This explains why wisdom is of the heart, not the mind. We gain wisdom through passion, love, caring, through giving and teaching and helping. We gain wisdom through God's Holy Spirit, which He places in our hearts when we are saved. What an amazing plan, and what an amazing God we serve. Let's use that wisdom God has given us to help someone today. After all, not everyone has wisdom, but everybody needs it.

**TIP**

Always fish the deepest end of fallen trees in the fall and late spring.

PHILIPPIANS 1:9

*This I pray, that your love may abound still more
and more in knowledge and all discernment.*

We've fished with lots of guides during our days on the water. Most were excellent and great folks to spend the day with. The key to success when fishing with guides is to follow their advice. Pretty simple, right? Not so fast. I guided all the way through college, knew the lake, knew the patterns, knew what fish were biting and where to catch them. Yet many paid little attention to what I told them. Almost all were older than me, and they figured they knew how to do it better.

As saved, born-again Christians, we have a Guide. His name is God. He even wrote a manual, called the Bible. Our Guide has all the knowledge, wisdom, and answers we will ever need in life. Our God is the secret to abounding in more love, knowledge, and discernment. Take His advice always!

**TIP**
Use a rattle in soft plastic to help the bass find your bait.

TITUS 2:2

*. . . that the older men be sober, reverent, temperate, sound in faith, in love, in patience.*

While speaking at sport shows, I've kidded the young boys about the qualities to look for when choosing a girlfriend. At the top of the list is to find a girl who loves (not likes) to fish. Today's scripture describes the perfect husband. So, if any of you ladies are looking, check some of these qualities before you start hanging out with the guys.

But how many of us guys qualify? Can I tell you? This is what God expects. And quite honestly, it's what He should expect—and what any woman should expect as well. Men, it just might be time for us to up our game. It's time to look at these attributes, examine ourselves, and see if we're lacking in one or some of these. God expects it. Women love it. Boys, it's time to man up and become who God created you to be!

**TIP**

Always look for differences when fishing a shoreline, such as pea gravel changing to chunk rock.

MATTHEW 5:44

*"But I say to you, love your enemies, bless those who curse you, do good to those who hate you, and pray for those who spitefully use you and persecute you."*

**A**rguments and disagreements have become commonplace in national bass tournaments. Generations clash as college-age kids compete against seasoned veterans like Ricky Clunn and Roland Martin. The younger pros could and should benefit greatly by learning respect and etiquette from the older guys.

Remember those "What Would Jesus Do?" bracelets and T-shirts? Well, today's verse came from Jesus Himself talking, so I think we should be pretty close on this one. Can we really love our enemies? Do good deeds to folks who hate us? How about pray for the very ones who use and abuse us? They lie to us, cheat, and steal, yet we're to pray for them and do them good? Want to be like Jesus? This is where it gets tough. Can you do it?

**TIP**
Heavy cover with deep water close by will provide all year long.

### JOSHUA 1:8

*"This Book of the Law shall not depart from your mouth, but you shall meditate in it day and night, that you may observe to do according to all that is written in it. For then you will make your way prosperous, and then you will have good success."*

Before heading out on a fishing trip, we make a list of items to make sure we have what we need. We certainly do this fishing tournaments, and it works pretty well. Ever go to the grocery store without a list and still bring back everything you needed? Me neither.

Our list for life is the Bible, God's living Word. In today's verse, God gave Joshua the keys to success: joy, prosperity, health, a long life, and unprecedented favor from God. It's all in there. All we need to do is speak, meditate, observe, and do what God wants us to do. I wonder what would happen if someone picked up the Bible, read it, and really lived by it!

**TIP**

When fishing suspended bass, it's better to keep your lure above the fish.

JIMMY HOUSTON

PSALM 46:10

*"Be still, and know that I am God; I will be exalted*
*among the nations, I will be exalted in the earth!"*

All fishermen are concerned about the big things in
fishing: boat, motor, electronics, trolling motor.
These are obviously important to success. But
it's the little things in everyday fishing that
make the difference: seeing a baitfish
jump, a small stickup, a dark spot under
the water, casting accuracy. Little things
are often the key to whether we catch fish
or not.

We often get so busy and wrapped up
with the little things in life that we leave
God out of most of it. Ever had a day where
God never really crossed your mind? Well, I
have. Maybe your first thought about God
was when you went to bed! I've been there and done that.
It's not a good feeling. Slow down, be still, and listen.
God wants to talk.

**TIP**
When shad
begin to die, try
a solid white
spinnerbait with
nickel blades.

PSALM 149:4

*The L*ORD *takes pleasure in His people; He will*
*beautify the humble with salvation.*

Fishermen love cloudy days; the lower visibility makes it easier to fish close to the fish. Fish have a tendency to stray farther away from cover. But in wintertime, we need sunshiny days. Not only is it better for you and me, but the fish welcome even a couple degrees change in water temp. Also, the sun gives better vision for the fish down deeper.

As we love sunshine in the winter, God loves His people. We are the apple of His eye. We are His most prized creation. Today's verse says God takes pleasure in the humble, those who consistently do the work of Jesus, go about it on a daily basis, and remain quiet about it. We all love a pat on the back every now and then. Sometimes we feel the need to do it ourselves. Resist that temptation. Zip it up and go about your business. God knows and will beautify us.

**TIP**

Add a small nail weight to sinking worms in deeper water.

JOB 13:15

*Though He slay me, yet will I trust Him. Even so,*
*I will defend my own ways before Him.*

We all know what a difference water temp makes to fish. Fish are cold-blooded creatures, so every little bit of change has an effect on them. It seems the temperature we can catch the most in shallow water is 58 degrees Fahrenheit. Amazingly, this is the magic temperature in both spring and fall.

What makes the biggest difference in a Christian's life? Jesus—and the closer we live our lives to Him, the more difference He will make in us. Today's verse is from Job. He had lost everything—his family, his livestock, his health and wealth. He was only left with his life and his wife. (But she despised him.) But still he trusted God and was sure of his righteousness and salvation. This is all God asks, all we need: trust, complete trust. Let's try a little Job-like trust and watch God work in our lives.

**TIP**

Deep standing timber is an ideal place to fish a jigging spoon.

### ECCLESIASTES 1:7

*All the rivers run into the sea, yet the sea is not full.*

River fishing is so much fun. It's almost totally shallow-water fishing. A key thing to remember is shallow does not necessarily mean close to the shoreline. The edges of long, shallow points often hold schools of bass. The ends of these may be five to ten feet deep and two or three hundred yards away from shore. A deep-diving crankbait is usually the ticket here. And don't forget to enjoy the beauty of the river.

It's amazing to me that anyone would not believe there is a God who created this wondrous and wonderful world we live in. Today's verse is an amazing and true statement written by King Solomon about three thousand years ago. He never saw the Mississippi or the Ohio Rivers, yet God inspired him to write this scripture. There definitely is a God, able to handle anything we encounter. Not only is He able; He is more than willing.

**TIP**

Accept the weather conditions and work with them.

MARK 11:24

*"Therefore I say to you, whatever things you ask when you pray, believe that you receive them, and you will have them."*

Grass retreats during the cold winter months. Grass that, earlier, came all the way or very near the surface now may be several feet deep. This is perfect. Just the same way it holds the water a little cooler in the summer, grass makes it a tad warmer in winter. A suspended jerkbait, lipless crank, or Mimic will bring bass out of the grass. Points, humps, and edges in the grass provide limitless spots to catch a fish.

Jesus was saying in today's verse that there are no limits to prayer. Whatever we ask for in a believing prayer, without a doubt, God will grant. This has always puzzled me, as I've prayed for many things without receiving them. I've come to realize that as a Christian I'm submitting to God's will, and my prayer must reflect that. The things I'm praying for must line up with God's will. Those things I always receive!

**TIP**
Fish lighter line and finesse baits on highly pressured lakes.

PSALM 32:8

*"I will instruct you and teach you in the way you should go; I will guide you with My eye."*

E lectronics have become the modern marvel in bass fishing. A GPS is available on everyone's boat, truck, or even our watches. It's awesome to be able to run down the lake at seventy miles per hour watching your boat on a GPS. Sure makes it easy to get back to your fishing hole and not get lost!

The Bible is God's GPS, and He's promised to lead us in the right direction. God has His eye on you and me. He helps with our decisions and choices. He talks to us through His Holy Spirit and won't ever let us lose our way as long as we listen and follow His guidance. God's Word is the key to success, great relationships, wisdom, joy, happiness, health, and even a long life. Let's listen to God today.

**TIP**

When water temps fall below 60 degrees Fahrenheit, bass get more aggressive.

JOHN 3:16

*"God so loved the world that He gave His only begotten Son, that whoever believes in Him should not perish but have everlasting life."*

Isn't it great that a bass's appetite is insatiable? Bass don't need to be hungry to strike our baits. They have what's called a reaction strike. Something comes inside their strike zone, or close to it, and they react by striking our bait.

We have a reaction strike too. Our reaction to this most famous of all scripture verses determines what our lives will be like all our days here on earth and throughout eternity. Eternal life or ever-lasting life is mentioned around fifty times in the New Testament, and it is speaking of a forever heaven. But it's also talking about the life we live with God today, tomorrow, next week, next year. It's our lives here on earth living God's Word, God's will, and all the abundance that comes with it! We need only believe in Jesus to have eternal life.

**TIP**

Never pass a piece of riprap without fishing it; fish will move on and off riprap all day.

PSALM 119:105

*Your word is a lamp to my feet and a light to my path.*

Before we had electronic maps, we used paper maps of all the lakes we fished. I probably have two or three hundred of these. One trick we used was to color in various bottom contours, usually at five or ten feet, in different colors. This would seemingly bring the map alive, and super-looking fishing spots would almost jump off the map. Most electronics allow us to do the same thing now, and it's a big aid in locating fish.

God's Word is like a map meant to lead you through any of life's problems or setbacks. God's Word has the contour lines colored so brightly! Just open His Bible anywhere and start reading. He will shed light on solutions to your circumstances. Believe me: I've done this many times. Open your Bible. Let God brighten your path, brighten your day, and brighten your life.

**TIP**
Use a stand-up jig head when keeping contact with the bottom.

JAMES 2:10

*Whoever shall keep the whole law, and yet
stumble in one point, he is guilty of all.*

Can old-fashioned lures work as well as the new ones? Remember the old hair or bucktail jig? Ironically, we have many new versions of hair jigs. I'd suggest trying some of the newer models on eight- to twelve-pound line on a seven- to eight-foot spinning rod. These become deadly when water temps fall below 45 degrees. Sometimes, old beats new.

> **TIP**
> Make the wind your friend. Fish windy banks and let the wind aid your casts.

What about those old rules in the Ten Commandments? Is adultery as bad a sin as murder? How about as bad as stealing? Is lying as bad as murder? In my human mind, it sure would be better to lie to someone than to kill him. James said in today's verse that all sin is the same to God. So if you're feeling pretty righteous today, don't. We are all sinners subject to judgment. But thankfully, if we have asked for God's mercy, we have it. And mercy triumphs over judgment.

DECEMBER

# DECEMBER 1

## 2 TIMOTHY 3:1

*Know this, that in the last days perilous times will come.*

The last day in any fishing tournament is always the most exciting. It's championship day. The top ten, twelve, or twenty are fishing for the big bucks. Fans are watching this week's cream of the crop in action. It's the same in every sport. That final game, final match, final chance to win, those are great days!

The last days Paul was telling young Timothy about in today's verse are right now, the age before Jesus makes His second appearance here on earth. Paul explained how men will be acting: as lovers of themselves and money, proud, blasphemous, unloving, unforgiving, traitors, unholy, and much more. Almost seems like Paul was describing much of America and the world right now. Of course, we are to be different. We are to be living the godly life God has designed for us. What will be perilous for the world will be glorious for us as we fly away.

**TIP**
Big flats with drainage ditches hold large populations of bass.

MATTHEW 16:24

*Jesus said to His disciples, "If anyone desires to come after Me,
let him deny himself, and take up his cross, and follow Me."*

I t only takes a little free time every now and
then to be a fisherman and have loads of
fun playing this great game. We don't need
to know much about fishing, and we all
start at some age with little or no knowledge.
Becoming a top-line pro tournament fisherman takes a ton of commitment, almost
beyond our capabilities. It takes complete
commitment. A commitment to learn and a
commitment of time.

**TIP**

Build your own
brush piles for
great bass and
crappie fishing.

Jesus first mentioned the cross to His
disciples earlier in Matthew. To these chosen disciples of Jesus, that was a picture of a
horrible, brutal, and degrading death. Was
Jesus actually asking for a commitment that included
such a physical death? Yes, He surely was; and He is
asking that same complete surrender from you and me.
This kind of faith, this kind of commitment, guarantees
eternal life. Jesus took up the cross for you and me!

## DECEMBER 3

GENESIS 12:1

*The LORD had said to Abram, "Get out of your country, from your family and from your father's house, to a land that I will show you."*

Pro fishing, like other pro sports, is a young man's game. Or is it? Roland Martin is fishing tournaments this year at eighty-one. Ricky Clunn is fishing them at seventy-four, and Gary Yamamoto at age seventy-seven. Don't ever think you're too old to accomplish great things or too old to make a difference in people's lives, or in the world, for that matter.

Abraham was seventy-five when God told him to pack his goods, his wife, his servants, and all his animals and head out. He had plenty and didn't need more possessions. He could have just sat back and enjoyed life. You know what happened? Abraham started an entire nation. By the way, Abraham had his son Isaac when he was a hundred! If God has put something in your mind and in your heart, do it, no matter what age you are.

> **TIP**
> Remember, structure or habitat is more important than depth.

EZEKIEL 2:2

*The Spirit entered me when He spoke to me.*

One of the key things to remember about crappie in the winter is that they layer in depths. What I mean is a school of crappie may be, say, around ten feet deep. The school will most likely be layered in a one-to-two-foot range, maybe eight to ten feet deep, or nine to eleven feet deep. All the fish are in the little one-to-two-foot window. Find that window and whack 'em! As they move up or down throughout the day, they stay in that small layer depth-wise.

God's power, on the other hand, has no boundaries. In the Old Testament, God selected certain individuals to be His prophets. When He did, God gave them power and protection to do the job He had for them. He empowered them by His Holy Spirit. I believe we receive that same power and protection by God's Holy Spirit when we get saved. We become God's prophets to a lost world.

> **TIP**
>
> Pink is a great color to catch crappie, especially in the winter.

PHILIPPIANS 4:6

*Be anxious for nothing, but in everything by prayer and supplication, with thanksgiving, let your requests be made known to God.*

It's almost impossible for a tournament fisherman not to worry, especially when we have found a big bunch of fish. Will they move? What if the weather changes? Who else might have found these fish or be on this pattern? Obviously, worry doesn't catch one single bass.

Paul said in this verse to worry about nothing. Why? Because worry shows a lack of trust in God and His power. But Paul also had the solution to worry. We humbly take it all to God in prayer, with thanksgiving in our hearts. We are asking God for solutions, not telling Him how we want our problems solved. Our worship, our gratitude, allows God to work wonders and perform miracles and give us a peace and tranquility that are hard to understand. We replace worry with worship and turn anxiety into thankfulness.

**TIP**
A thinner line on your locator screen signifies a hard bottom.

PHILIPPIANS 4:7

*The peace of God, which surpasses all understanding, will
guard your hearts and minds through Christ Jesus.*

A trick I learned from one of my Kansas fishing and
hunting buddies, Dennis Hamel, is well worth learning for anyone having trouble with backlashes or teaching
a youngster or a new fisherman how to throw a bait-
casting reel. Simply make a long cast; then add a single
piece of tape around your spool. Now,
wind the line back in and begin casting
lessons. No backlash can go beyond
that single piece of tape.

**TIP**
Fish deeper
steep
points with
crankbaits
as the water
cools.

God's peace is that piece of tape on the
backlashes of life. It settles us in Him through
whatever goes wrong in our lives. Our devo-
tion yesterday tells us how to get this peace by
giving God the backlash with thanksgiving
and not worrying. Sound impossible? It is in
human terms. But God can give you peace
unsurpassed in every backlash. And He will!
Give God a chance today.

# DECEMBER 7

LUKE 9:3

*"Take nothing for the journey, neither staffs nor bag nor bread nor money."*

A s we reach the end of another year, let's look at two baits, both extremely easy to fish, that will produce almost any time of the year. First, a wacky worm—a sinking worm hooked in the middle, on a small hook and light line. Simply let it fall. The other is a small- to medium-size deep-diving crank-bait, like my American Originals Deep Smoothy. We can catch bass anywhere with these two baits.

We need even less to catch a better life. When we come into this world, we bring nothing. When we depart to either heaven or hell, we take nothing. Jesus, in today's verse, was sending out His chosen disciples with nothing other than His gospel and the power and authority that comes with it. Whatever we achieve, whatever we accomplish, whatever we acquire means nothing. All that matters is our relationship with Jesus and His resurrection power to carry us to heaven.

> **TIP**
> Add as little action as possible to a wacky worm in clear water.

JIMMY HOUSTON

JAMES 2:13

*Judgment is without mercy to the one who has shown no mercy. Mercy triumphs over judgment.*

Being a tournament director is a no-win position in most cases. The director wants all competitors to succeed yet must enforce all the rules fairly and, at times, disqualify some.

How difficult it must be for an almighty God, whose desire is for all to be saved, to watch mankind reject His laws and principles and ultimately reject Him. He must also deal fairly with each of us. In today's verse, James was explaining that those who show no mercy to others must fall into judgment. This judgment is hell. Our compassion to others is proof of our acceptance of God's mercy to us. Our lives should be filled with mercy and com-passion for others. This shows God, and the world, that we have received God's mercy that is totally victorious over judgment. We will have that chance today to show mercy.

**TIP**
Creek channels form underwater highways for bass. Find stopping areas.

PSALM 139:2

*You know my sitting down and my rising up;*
*You understand my thought afar off.*

How would we react if we knew everything there was to know about bass or crappie or catfish? How about walleye, trout, all the saltwater fish? Well, certainly we could catch them better. We would always know where they were and what they were thinking.

Get this: God knows this about you and me. In today's verse, David was blown away, and we should be as well, to realize God knows all this (even David's—and our—very next sin) and loves us anyway. There is nothing we can do or say or even think that is hidden from God. It is scary knowing our faults and shortcomings. How could we ever please God? We please Him with our hearts. God looks inside our hearts. Whatever is there, good or evil, is what is important to Him. *Lord, create in me a pure heart!*

**TIP**

The nastier the weather, the better the smallmouth bite.

GALATIANS 3:27

*As many of you as were baptized into Christ have put on Christ.*

Many people fish a trailer on a spinnerbait all the time, adding a twin tail trailer or curly tail grub. I prefer to fish a spinnerbait with no trailer attached, unless I'm missing fish. If the bass are missing my bait or hitting it with their mouths closed, that's when I add on a trailer, usually a twin tail. This seems to solve the problem.

In the verse for today, the apostle Paul, Christianity's greatest missionary, was not adding anything to Jesus in order to "catch" new Christians. Our goal is to live, act, and react just as Christ would. We have become united with Jesus Christ when we become a part of the crucifixion and resurrection of Jesus. Can we do this? Can we put on Christ to a lost and dying world? I believe we can because through Jesus we have been given His righteousness. Let's show that righteousness today and every day.

**TIP**
A loop knot will give a crankbait or stickbait more action.

**PROVERBS 22:23**

*The LORD will plead their cause, and plunder*
*the soul of those who plunder them.*

During FLW Tour events on our off days, the Wednesdays between official practice and actual competition, competitors got together to do a wonderful activity: volunteer community service. We usually had twenty to twenty-five of us competitors volunteer in each town we visited. We served the homeless and disabled, visited children's hospitals, and met a lot of good people. They helped us maybe even more than we were helping them.

Today's proverb is specifically about the poor and afflicted. In biblical times, they sat at the city gates and at temple doors. Jesus said we will always have the poor among us (Matthew 26:11). This verse tells us how important the poor and afflicted are to God. They're so important we put our own souls in danger by taking advantage of them. We are never to neglect the poor and should always look for ways to help them. God created us all.

**TIP**

Boat docks will hold crappie all winter.

GENESIS 15:1

*"Do not be afraid, Abram. I am your shield,
your exceedingly great reward."*

**W**intertime fishing scares most fishermen. Fish are cold-blooded, and most don't bite as well in cold temps. Obviously, most of us don't like to be cold either. These days, we have excellent winter clothing to protect us from the cold. With that cold-weather protection shielding me against the elements, I usually switch from bass to crappie for wintertime fishing.

**TIP**

Noisier baits tend to work better early in the morning and right before dark.

Today's verse tells us God is our protection and shield against whatever comes our way. God spoke these words to Abram after he had rescued his nephew Lot; and they sum up why we need a personal relationship with God. He's able to replace our fear with His amazing powers—faith over fear. He's our protector all the days of our lives. Plus, God rewards us with His exceedingly great blessings. What an awesome God we serve!

JOHN 3:17

*"God did not send His Son into the world to condemn the world, but that the world through Him might be saved."*

Bass fishing is mostly catch-and-release fishing. Most of us will spend extra time to revive a fish. We add ice and chemicals to our live wells and turn on the oxygen pump all to save one bass.

God did much more to save us. It's even more exciting to watch God work in your life, to see Him get involved in your problems and circumstances, and to see Him put the right people in place to help. I've seen God put together a whole string of events just to get me where I need to be. I'll be honest: I've seen God do so many remarkable things in my life that I can't wait to see what He's about to do next. God can just keep making it better and better.

**TIP**

Buy your kids and spouse or girlfriend/ boyfriend good fishing equipment.

ECCLESIASTES 3:11

*He has made everything beautiful in its time.*
*Also He has put eternity in their hearts.*

We all fight time in our lives. We live in the busiest, most hurry-up country in the world. I have constantly lived a horrendous schedule, doing thirty-nine television shows, over a hundred personal appearances, and more than five hundred videos a year for YouTube and Facebook—plus a complete B.A.S.S. or FLW Tournament schedule. How is this possible? By putting God and family first in my schedule and in my life. My motto: I have all the time to do all God intends me to do this year. Chris and I include family in everything. Whatever we are doing and wherever we are is in God's plans, and it's beautiful. We are walking together with God and our family in all we do. And we know for sure that this journey will continue into eternity! God has put that desire and assurance of eternity in our hearts as proof our family will walk together forever.

**TIP**

If you have color shading on your sonar mapping, use it!

HEBREWS 1:3

*[Christ,] when He had by Himself purged our sins, sat down at the right hand of the Majesty on high.*

Casting accuracy comes from making literally hundreds of thousands, if not millions, of casts. We develop a muscle memory that allows us to make great casts, time after time. This same muscle memory works on the retrieve of a lure and can really limit how many strikes we get. Concentrate on changing retrieve speed and cadence so you will get more bites. Change can be good!

**TIP**
Pay attention to small details when reading the weather, such as wind direction and cloud cover.

The best change we can ever experience is when God changes our lives from death to life. His Son, Jesus, was crucified on a cross and covered our sins with His precious blood. His sacrifice makes us pure in God's sight. When you and I repent of our sins and ask God to become our Lord and Savior, our sins are gone! Jesus Himself is seated on that mighty throne to one day look at His Father and say, "This one's mine."

ISAIAH 12:2

*Behold, God is my salvation, I will trust and not be afraid.*

Instinct (or gut feeling, as us rednecks call it) is important in all sports, but especially in fishing. I believe instinct is another gift from God to help us live abundant and joyful lives. Follow your instincts. They often will stop you on the best spot to fish and guide you to use the right technique and pick out the number one lure in your tackle box. Don't be afraid to follow that gut feeling. It's often the road to a successful fishing day.

Our instinct to trust God must overcome fear, which might be the number one lure in the devil's tackle box. We saw fear run rampant during the coronavirus as Christians traded faith for fear. We know faith is not easy. Fear is a piece of cake. God's prophets lived in constant danger of losing their lives proclaiming God's Word. You and I must realize what they knew: death is temporary. Life eternal is forever when we trust God.

**TIP**
Steep bluff banks produce in clear, cold lakes in the winter.

# DECEMBER 17

GENESIS 15:6

*He believed in the L*ORD*, and He accounted*
*it to him for righteousness.*

The key to catching wintertime bass seems to be depth. Ironically one lake may have bass at twenty to twenty-five feet while in another lake nearby, the bass might be at twelve to fifteen feet. It is vital to figure out what depth most of the bass are located. With today's fish finders, we actually see the fish. Seeing is believing. Now we catch 'em!

As Christians, it's vital for you and me to believe—to believe God's words, to believe His promises, and to believe His Son, Jesus, died for our sins. We need to believe Jesus walked out of that grave to prove forever that He had power over death. That's how we become righteous before God. We believe no enemy can harm us. No person, no government power, no devil. You and I must trust God when there is no way because He is the way, and all our hope! I'm a believer.

**TIP**
Diving seagulls are a dead giveaway for schools of shad.

PROVERBS 15:1

*A soft answer turns away wrath, but a harsh word stirs up anger.*

Over the years I've had the honor of learning from most of the best fishermen ever, from greats like Roland Martin; my wife, Chris; Larry Nixon; Hank Parker; Ricky Clunn; Tommy Martin; and Bill Dance. I could fill this page with names. I remember telling Kevin VanDam one day at weigh-in, "I thought about that but didn't try it." Kevin gently replied, "If you think it, do it." Kevin's answer was from the heart and forever helpful.

> **TIP**
> Volunteer to help in local youth fishing events.

Today's proverb is so easy to understand and true almost every time. Yet we violate it time after time. How many arguments could we totally avoid with a simple soft answer? How many do we escalate by just the opposite? I don't think giving a soft answer is easy, and it definitely requires conscious effort on our part to make it happen. Today, when the opportunity arises to give a soft answer, let's do it! Bless your heart.

# DECEMBER 19

PSALM 4:7

*You have put gladness in my heart, more than in the*
*season that their grain and wine increased.*

The biggest bass are generally in the very thickest of cover most of the time. During the year, many anglers miss catching really big bass by not fishing right in the middle of the meanest, thickest stuff you can find. It's always best to fish the edges of cover first, but always bow up and make that final cast or two deep in the heart of the thickest stuff available.

What God has put deep in the heart of every believer is gladness. This joy is better than whatever great things God may bless us with. In other words, this gladness, this happiness, is not dependent on something good happening. This joy is available and present during bad times just as much as in good. Our gladness comes from that close, personal relationship with God, regardless of what's happening around us.

ACTS 2:24

*God raised up [Jesus], having loosed the pains of death,*
*because it was not possible that He should be held by it.*

Many winter tournaments are won on crankbaits. Don't think you need to always be cranking slow. One of the best techniques in cold water is speed cranking a crankbait. If grass is available, use a bait that gets close to, but won't quite touch, the grass. In lakes without grass, use the deep divers, but still crank them fast—and don't forget to stop every few feet. Speed crank and beat that cold water!

In today's verse, the good doctor Luke explained the victory Jesus attained over death by walking out of that grave. It's that same victory you and I claim over death by believing in and making Jesus our Lord and Savior. This victory for you and me is one basic tenet of Christianity and is proof positive for what we believe: we have life abundantly here on earth and life eternal with Jesus when we leave.

**TIP**
Pay special attention and slow down anytime your bait bumps into something.

## JOHN 14:15

*"If you love Me, keep My commandments."*

One of the keys to becoming a better fish catcher this coming year is to decide to follow the fish throughout their yearly movement patterns. Soon, when winter is the coldest, bass will concentrate at the bottom of creeks near bends and points. As the water warms, follow those fish to points, nearby spawning areas, then into a summer pattern, then a fall pattern. Eventually you're right back where we are right now! The more you learn about how to follow these movements, the more bass you will catch.

If we want to follow Jesus in our daily lives as we walk this earth, we must love Him and keep His commandments. Loving Jesus is easy when we understand He died on the cross, a cruel, horrible, painful death, to pay the price for every sin you and I would ever commit. He gave His closest disciples very simple advice: *If you love Me, keep my commandments.*

**TIP**

Outside bends in creeks generally have washed-out undercut banks from current that bass love and use to hide and ambush food.

MATTHEW 5:8

*Blessed are the pure in heart, for they shall see God.*

L ooking for a fun-filled day fishing in the winter? Watch the weather forecast and pick out sunny days. Not the sunny day following a cold front, but the last day after two or three sunny days and ahead of the next cold front. You get super fishing with days in the fifties and hopefully low sixties. Whack 'em!

As the warm sun blesses us with good fishing, God blesses us with His favor. We are happy, joyful, fortunate. We realize this comes from our relationship with God. This is not a happiness that folks seek through riches, fame, power, or worldly goods. This is a constant joy and happiness during all circumstances, good and bad. When our hearts are pure and line up with God's, we are truly very blessed. Let's work on making our hearts pure before God.

**TIP**

When deciding where to fish deep in the winter, imagine draining the lake. Fish where the last water would be.

PSALM 16:11

*In Your presence is fullness of joy; at Your right hand are pleasures forevermore.*

My choices for wintertime bass fishing don't include lots of baits. I want something that resembles a shad or school of shad; an umbrella rig or Alabama rig with three to five shad baits; a deep-diving crankbait, like an American Originals Deep Smoothy in shad color; or a bait with secondary action, like a jig that pulsates or with a trailer that moves when still or worked slowly.

My choice for everyday life—fullness of joy! Throughout the psalms, David spoke of joy with God over and over. David had it tough before and after he became king. He was betrayed by friends and family, hunted down, homeless, lied to, and falsely accused, and he failed often. He even committed grievous sins. Despite all this, David chose joy with the God he served. I'm choosing joy today. I'm choosing pleasure forevermore with my God. How about you?

**TIP**

Fish an umbrella rig on a 6'9"–7'3" medium-heavy action rod.

2 CORINTHIANS 5:1

*We know that if our earthly house, this tent, is*
*destroyed, we have a building from God, a house*
*not made with hands, eternal in the heavens.*

We have learned a great deal by video game fishing, which is real fishing done using a LiveScope that allows us to see fish under the water and around our boat. Can it get any better than this? We have discovered that we are better off fishing our lure over the fish as opposed to under them. We've known forever to bring our spinnerbaits over the top of brush, logs, stumps, and grass to get the bass to come up and eat them. Well, the same is true down deeper as well.

**TIP**
Trout fishing is best during the colder months.

We can't see heaven now on any fish finder, but our joy, our confidence, our trust in God comes from knowing this life here on earth is only temporary. On a glassy lake at sunset, I can almost see, almost feel heaven, my permanent home! Jesus has indeed prepared many mansions. One of them is mine. One is yours! Imagine heaven when problems pop up today.

LUKE 2:11

*For there is born to you this day in the City of
David, a Savior, who is Christ the Lord.*

Not many folks are fishing Christmas Day. It's a day
set aside by most as a family day for celebrating the
birth of Jesus. We have home-
cooked meals and exchange gifts.
The last week of the year is still
strong fishing. My fishing buddy Josh Jones
caught his personal best biggest a couple
of days after Christmas. Many miss out on
this great time period to catch giant bass.

Most folks at the time Jesus was born
missed out on a key part of today's verse—
"There is born to you . . . a Savior!" Many
today still miss this most important fact.
Jesus left heaven to save a dying world. God
loves us so much He sent Jesus to save you and me. As
you eat more than you should today and open more gifts
than you probably deserve, remember Jesus, your Savior!

LUKE 6:35

*Love your enemies, do good, and lend, hoping for*
*nothing in return; and your reward will be great.*

One of the quickest ways to get to deep cold-water fish is with a spoon. A heavy Hopkins or CC Spoon or slab in chrome, white, or chartreuse drops to the bottom like a bullet and can fish twenty to sixty feet of water quickly and effectively. Not that difficult.

Pleasing God is not that difficult either: do good to those who have done us wrong. We return their bad with good we get from God. The God we serve is a rewarding God. He rewards us when we reward others, even when they have harmed us or they are our enemies. Loving those who love us is its own reward, but God seems to really pay attention when we love and help those who don't love us back. Maybe that tells God how big our hearts really are! Now, that is an effective way to please God!

TIP

Fish under piles of floating dead leaves in tail ends of small pockets or coves.

PROVERBS 15:4

*A wholesome tongue is a tree of life.*

We use barbless hooks exclusively when fishing the lakes here on our ranch. We release most all of the fish we catch, and obviously barbless hooks do very little damage to the fish. One little trick: if you hook a fish in the tongue and it starts to bleed, pour soda pop on the wound to stop the bleeding and save the fish's life. Most fish prefer Mountain Dew.

Our tongues, when used properly, can literally be life-giving to those we come in contact with every day. God didn't create our tongues to gossip or tear down but to edify and lift up. They're not meant to curse but to bless. Imagine what America and our world would be like if politicians and the media could talk without running down their opposition or America. Before we amen that, let's be very careful we don't let the devil drag our own tongues into that trap.

**TIP**

Black, blue, and purple is a perfect color combination for a jig.

1 PETER 1:18–19

*You were not redeemed with corruptible things, like silver or gold . . . but with the precious blood of Christ.*

Blade colors on spinnerbaits can be very important at times. A good place to start is with a single gold blade or gold as your end blade, combined with nickel or silver on the shaft. Try nickel blades in clear water, gold in dingy. In really muddy water, white blades seem to be more visible. It's your choice.

More important than choosing spinner blade colors, we can choose to love God and accept His Son, Jesus, as our Lord and Savior—or not. He has redeemed us and paid for our sins with His blood. But we can turn that down if we choose. If you're saved today, praise God. If not, God won't twist your arm or force you to obey. You know His promises. You know the consequences. The choice is yours and mine to make.

**TIP**

If bass are missing your spinnerbait, add a soft plastic trailer.

## DECEMBER 29

JEREMIAH 10:10

*The LORD is the true God; He is the living*
*God and the everlasting King.*

The key to fishing big lakes is to make them smaller. Concentrate on just one or two bays or pick a major creek and learn all you can about that area. Remember: the fish that live there generally spend their entire lives in that one creek or bay. Their range is small.

How big, really, is the God we serve? And how much does He really love us? Well, He's bigger than we can ever imagine. We have a tendency to make God smaller at times. He's so big that He flung billions of stars into space and created oceans and every living thing. He intricately created you and me and gave us dominion over all He created. Yet He loved us so much, He stepped out of heaven to be humiliated, tortured, and killed just to keep you and me from going to hell. That's how big He is, and that's how much He loves us!

**TIP**
Search out schools of shad on long points.

PSALM 42:1

*As the deer pants for the water brooks, so
pants my soul for You, O God.*

Our pet deer, Lucy, and her amazing herd require a lot
of water every day. We actually keep an ice chest on
the deck all summer and let it drip to keep their water
bowl full. Plus, we keep another three-gallon container at
the end of the house *and* they have a large
lake handy to drink from. These deer
won't last long without water.

Our souls are in trouble without a
good daily watering by God. We get this by
talking with Him (prayer) and by spending
time in His Word (the Bible). Jesus offers us
living water (John 7:38). This water guarantees satisfaction through all eternity for
our souls. When your life seems a bit empty,
problems mount, and you have no answers,
turn to God to satisfy your soul. God will
soothe your soul and save your life.

**TIP**
Fish the
edges of a
brush pile
first; then
fish the
heart of it.

PROVERBS 13:20
*He who walks with wise men will be wise, but*
*the companion of fools will be destroyed.*

Tournament fishermen are fiercely and individually competitive. Yet they will share their most secret lure and fishing information with a handful of their buddies—ones they are sure they can trust.

Today's proverb tells us how powerful our association with others can become. It's letting us know we will become like the folks we run around with. This can be very positive and good or extremely harmful to the point of destruction. Many men and women are in actual prisons today because of the company they keep. Others are chained to addictions and bad habits for the same reasons. Examine the friends you have! Are they encouraging, helpful, upbeat, and cheering you on? Or are they pulling you down? Sometimes a relationship could be keeping us from becoming all God meant us to be. Take a look at those you're walking with today.

**TIP**
Single standing trees hold giant bass all winter.